D1174062

HANDMADE SILK FLOWERS

HANDMADE
S·I·L·K
FLOWERS

Bruce W. Miller
Mary C. Donnelly

Prentice Hall Press · New York

To our parents,
whose enthusiasm has always sustained us

Published by Prentice Hall Press
A Division of Simon & Schuster, Inc.

PRENTICE HALL PRESS is a trademark of Simon & Schuster, Inc.

Library of Congress Cataloging in Publication Data

Miller, Bruce W.
  Handmade silk flowers.
  Bibliography
  Includes index.
  1. Silk flowers.   1. Donnelly, Mary
C. II. Title.
TT890.7.M55 1985   745.594'3   84-20924
ISBN: 0-671-60731-6

Manufactured in the United States of America

10 9 8 7 6 5 4 3 2 1

CONTENTS

PREFACE

Flowers have always had the power to arrest our attention. From the fragile and airy profusion of spring plum blossoms to the unfolding elegance of the long-stemmed rose, man has sought to preserve the ephemeral qualities of the flower. Silk flowers have the best qualities of the original, captured and held fast to be enjoyed in any season.

It was the Victorians who labored to give these qualities names and to place them within a specific panoply of meaning. The Victorians were not the first to give flowers special meanings, however: The ancient Greeks were well known for giving flora meaning and significance apart from its natural beauty. Still, it was not until the nineteenth century in Britain that "flower language" developed into a cult. Most flower language was adapted from the French classic *Le Langage des Fleurs* by Madame de la Tour, published around 1840. The Victorians, who were serious gardeners, would convey messages by including flowers with particular connotations in floral bouquets; in this fashion many a maid was courted.

When making silk flowers, think of yourself as endowing your flower with the qualities of the original. That marvelous resemblance to life, that uncanny ability to bring forth a remembrance, an evocation, are what make silk flowers so attractive. This book is about our pursuit of those ephemeral and wonderful qualities that make the flower a joy to see. We hope you find some pleasure and beauty here.

ACKNOWLEDGMENTS

We acknowledge and are grateful for the excellent previous work in this field by the following people: Yuri Uchiyama, Miyuki and Tomoko Iida, Vera Jeffery and Malcolm Lewis, Betty Valle, Burt and Patty Trick.

We would further like to acknowledge Sonoko Tsuchiya, whose generous explanation of some techniques and processes helped make this a better book, and Steve Brown of the San Luis Obispo Floral Design Studio for his arrangements of our flowers.

INTRODUCTION

The word *silk* conjures up images of the expensive or even the exotic, yet man has been making and using the fabric for centuries. It first appeared in China, where, for more than a thousand years, the Chinese guarded the secret of sericulture, or silkmaking. During that time sericulture reached a high degree of perfection, a beautiful art that remained mysterious to Westerners.

The secret of silk, of course, is the silkworm. From ancient to modern times, the silkworm has been tended carefully, feeding on the leaves of the white mulberry tree, until it reaches the cocoon stage—for it is the cocoon that is the source of silk. The worm secretes two types of filament from its mouth—one is silk and the other is a glutinous, or gummy, substance. These several filaments combine and dry in the air, forming a single long strand from which the worm makes its cocoon. It takes about seventy-two hours for the silkworm to produce the cocoon out of the single continuous filament—which measures anywhere from 600 to 1,200 yards. In ten to fifteen days, the silkworm will hatch and become a moth; before that happens, the cocoons are gathered and steamed and hung out to dry. If the pupa is allowed to hatch, it will ruin the cocoon. Some moths are allowed to hatch for breeding purposes, and the silk that remains in these damaged cocoons is made into short fibers to produce spun silk.

After the cocoons are harvested, the next step in silkmaking is to take the dried undamaged cocoons and boil them. This softens the sericin, the gum that holds the cocoon together. The single strand can now be unwound for its entire length. This unwound filament is raw silk; the process of unwinding is known as reeling. Raw silk is rough and without luster because it still has a great deal of gum on it. The remaining gum is removed by boiling the raw silk in soapy water.

The degummed silk, now a long, translucent fiber, is then twisted with another strand to form a thrown, or double, silk thread, which is wound onto skeins for use.

Cultivated silk is a soft, resilient, lightweight fiber. It is white in color and naturally smooth to the touch. Wild silk, on the other hand, comes from worms that do not feed exclusively on mulberry leaves, and it tends to be darker in color—usually light brown or tan. Silk, being a natural product, has a great affinity for dyes. There are as many as 300 different colors of silk thread.

Silk has always been considered one of the finest fabrics available, and it can be used in a multitude of ways. Its luxurious —almost regal—look has made it the fabric of choice for many people. Silk is used for clothing, for needlework, for upholstery— and for elegant handmade flowers. Silk is the fabric of choice for handmade flowers because it readily accepts dye and is easily shaped with tools. Moreover, its natural luster contributes to the beauty of the handmade flower.

Handmade Silk Flowers is a step-by-step guide to the creation of silk flowers. Anyone, from the novice to the experienced craftsperson, can use the instructions in this book. No special skills are required for making silk flowers. The tools and materials are relatively inexpensive, and most of the techniques and processes are easy to carry out. The resulting flowers are spectacular examples of the creative and the functional.

Silk flowers can be used in a variety of ways, from wedding bouquets to dining-table centerpieces. They make excellent gifts (for who is not cheered by the sight of a lovely flower?), and although nothing can replace the natural charm of a real flower, silk flowers have a special beauty and appeal all their own. What's more, a silk flower will last forever.

Part I of *Handmade Silk Flowers* covers all the information you need to get started— tools and materials as well as the basic techniques and processes used for the flowers in this book. Part II contains instructions and illustrations for making forty-four flowers. To make this book easy

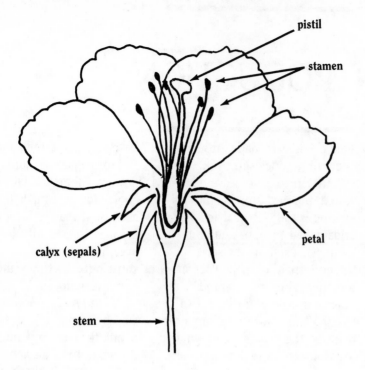

pistil

stamen

petal

calyx (sepals)

stem

0-1. The parts of a flower.

to use, each chapter includes everything from a close-up photograph to a list of materials to the full-size patterns for the particular flower. Part III is a special section devoted to wedding flowers. For those who want to read even more about the subject of silk flowers, the bibliography contains a number of helpful books and pamphlets.

Before you start your first project, we suggest that you become familiar with the parts of a flower (see fig. 0-1). You will more easily understand the assembly instructions if you understand the basic structures of any flower. Then read the first two chapters carefully. These will acquaint you with what's ahead—and get your flowermaking off to a good start.

· PART I ·
THE
BASICS

CHAPTER 1

TOOLS AND MATERIALS

You can buy and use many specialized tools for making silk flowers, but for the most part, you can make use of tools you already have on hand. If you want to invest in the specialized equipment such as that shown in figure 1-1, visit stores that handle supplies for Japanese arts and crafts. You will find, however, that the tools listed below, which are common household items, can be used quite effectively. All these tools are used for some or all of the flowers included in this book.

awl
dinner knives (without serrated
    edge)
small, sharp scissors
wire cutter
needlenosed pliers
brushes—sumi-e (Japanese
    watercolor) or other artists'
    brushes
ruler
felt-tipped pens or colored
    markers
heavy foam rubber (6 inches by 6
    inches by 1 inch) or skin
    diver's neoprene
electric hot plate
heavy newsprint (to use as blot-
    ting paper)
sewing needle
small bowls for dyeing
tweezers

In addition to the tools, silk flowermaking requires the use of relatively few materials that are

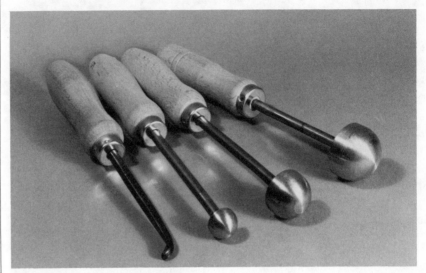

1-1. Japanese tools for ironing silk flowers.

obtained easily. These include silk, other fabrics, starch or sizing, dyes, glue, floral tape, wide green satin ribbon, and wire. You will also need absorbent cotton, white tissue paper, carbon paper, construction paper, cardboard, thread, and cheesecloth.

If you plan to make your own flower centers, you can select from a wide variety of additional materials. Flower centers are an aspect of flowermaking in which you can be particularly creative with materials (fig. 1-2). The flower center is a small but important part of your silk flower —it provides authenticity and subtle delicacy. Almost every flower species has its own distinct center.

Ready-made flower centers, in a variety of colors and sizes, are

available at well-stocked craft or hobby shops. Usually you can also find plain white stamens that have been made from thread or covered wire. You can dye these to suit your particular flower.

If you cannot find commercial flower centers—or if you prefer to make your own—there are literally thousands of potential substitutes. (See "Making Stamens" in Chapter 2.) You can make stamens from wire, either plain or wrapped with tissue paper; you can make a pistil from a short length of wire bent back upon itself in a loop and then wrapped in a teardrop shape. You can use any number of kinds of string, thread, sisal twine, or jute. (Sisal twine is excellent.) You can separate or unravel these and then twist them into the proper

3

1-2. *Flower centers.*

shape. (Do not forget that starch and dye can also be put to good use here.)

You can also make flower centers from fabric or crepe paper. Crepe paper is usually rolled or twisted. When cut into a strip and fringed along one edge (fig. 1-3), fabric makes a good center for marguerites and other daisylike flowers. (You then roll the strip into a cylinder and splay it apart from the center outward to form the flower center, as shown in figure 1-4.) Bread dough, pipe cleaners, beads, buttons, dried flower parts, and seeds are all options for flower-center materials.

Examine the center of the real flower you plan to duplicate —and then experiment with whatever you have around the house.

Fabrics

The primary fabric used for the flowers in this book is, of course, silk. While every one of the flowers has at least *some* silk

in it, other fabrics are needed to produce the finished product. These hand-crafted flowers are always referred to as silk flowers, however, because their major ingredient is silk—and perhaps, too, because the word *silk* has always been attached to something of value, something elegant.

We have found that plain white China silk, available in any good fabric store, is the best kind of silk to use. This white silk allows you the greatest control over colors, because you do the dyeing yourself. Because silk is a natural material, it readily

accepts a great variety of dyes. Real (100 percent) silk is, in fact, unusually receptive to dyeing and can be purchased in a startling number of colors. This commercially dyed silk is also effective in making your silk flowers. You will need about ¼ yard of silk to produce two or three large flowers.

Cotton is the next-most-common fabric used in flower-making. It tends to be rougher and stiffer than silk and also readily accepts sizing and dyes. Because of its rougher texture, cotton is often used to make the leaves of silk flowers. The best cotton to use is a thin, white, evenly woven variety. Other fabrics occasionally used include chiffon, organza, rayon, rayon velvet, velveteen georgette, crepe de chine, and wide satin ribbon. Many of these fabrics, however, are synthetic and will not accept dyes or, in many cases, the starch sizing.

One important tip for selecting your fabric, especially velvet, is to take a small bottle of sizing or water to the fabric store to test on a tiny sample of the fabric that you are considering buying. (Be sure to ask the store clerk for a swatch.) If the fabric does not absorb the starch or water readily, it will be unsatisfactory for your needs.

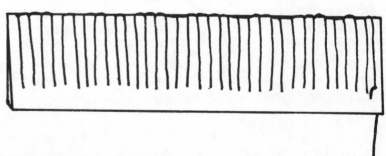

1-3. *Fabric strip with doubled wire at the end.*

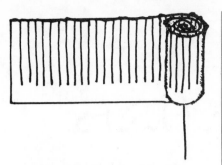

1-4. *Form a flower center by rolling up the fabric strip.*

Starch or Sizing

Starch or sizing stiffens the fabric and makes it retain its shape after it is molded. Many of the flowers in this book are made with starched fabric. The starch also keeps edges from fraying, although this is also accomplished when you cut your fabric on the bias. Sizing is made in several ways as well as in several consistencies. Try different types of starch or sizing in different consistencies for the different fabrics you use and the different flowers you make. Use the type and consistency that best enable your fabric to resemble the shape of the real flower you are making. Tulips, for example, should be stiffer than pansies.

In general, fabric starch with white glue makes a fine sizing. Cornstarch cooked down to a thick paste with water and white glue will also do. Aerosol starch can be used for making rolled-edge silk flowers.

Dyes

The array of dyes available is so large that you can duplicate almost any flower color. Dyes are divided into two categories—commercial and natural. Commercial, or aniline, dyes tend to be stronger and more stable because their colors are fixed. Commercial dyes that are effective for making silk flowers are SeriTint, Tinfix, New Milling Colours, Dylon Cold, and any Japanese cold-water dyes used for painting on fabrics.

Natural dyes, even when fixed with a mordant (a chemical that fixes the colors of dyes), tend to be fugitive (likely to change or fade). On the other hand, a natural dye often will produce some of the most beautiful and subtle hues—colors that seem to give the fabric an ephemeral, lifelike quality. The use of natural dyes is

an art in itself. More information on them appears in several books listed in the bibliography at the back of this book.

Glue

We recommend white Sobo glue for making silk flowers, although you can use any white glue that is suitable for fabrics. However, if you are making rolled-edge flowers (see Chapter 2), Sobo glue is a must because of its thick consistency.

Floral Tape

Floral tape, which comes in a wide variety of colors, is covered with a waxy substance (fig. 1-5). It is used for wrapping and attaching flower parts (leaves, sepals, and flowers) to the stem of the flower. Craft stores generally stock floral tape.

Wire

Wire is categorized by gauge, which refers to its diameter or thickness. When glued to a petal or used as a stem, wire gives the flower structure and support. You will also be using thin cloth-covered wire for supporting parts of leaves and petals that will be visible on the finished flower. This cloth-covered wire comes in a variety of colors, but you can also buy white cloth-covered wire and dye it to the needed color at the same time that you are dyeing the leaves and petals.

For flower stems you will need a variety of gauges of wire, depending on the weight of the flower and how much structure you need to provide. The most common sizes of wire available at craft or hardware stores are (from thinnest to thickest): #30, #24, #20, #18, and #16.

1-5. *Floral tape for wrapping flower stems.*

CHAPTER 2

TECHNIQUES AND PROCESSES

*N*ow that you have gathered together the tools and purchased the necessary materials that you will need for your first project, it's time to run through the various techniques used in silk flowermaking. After selecting the flower you want to make, you will trace and cut the patterns, starch your fabric (if the directions call for it), dye the fabric (unless you have purchased commercially dyed fabric), attach wire to leaves and petals, shape the parts of the flower, make flower centers and buds, and assemble your flower or group of flowers. You may also want to try some of the special effects discussed at the end of this chapter.

Cutting Your Patterns

After choosing the flower you plan to make, look at the patterns for it. All of the patterns are drawn to actual size. Now examine the fabric you have selected and determine the direction of the grain (the way the fabric tears most easily). You will be cutting all of your fabric on the bias (diagonal to the grain), so the diagonal length of the pattern (shown on each pattern with an arrow) must be placed parallel to the grain of the material. (See fig. 2-1.)

There are several ways to transfer the full-size pattern from the page to your fabric. If your fabric is sheer (as most silk is), place it directly over the pattern and trace with a blunt pencil

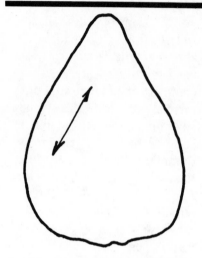

2-1. The arrow must be parallel to the grain of the fabric.

directly on the fabric. A second way to transfer a pattern is to place your fabric underneath the pattern, with dressmaker's carbon in between. Then move a pencil along the printed pattern; a carbon copy will appear on your fabric.

If you are mass-producing one flower type, make templates —cardboard or construction-paper patterns—from the original pattern. Once fashioned, these templates (one for each part of the flower) can be used to trace many flower parts rapidly and will not wear out.

Once you become proficient at silk flowermaking, you will undoubtedly want to make flowers for which there are no available patterns. This should not be a problem, since you can, with little effort, create your own patterns.

To make your own patterns from scratch, you might try just taking a very close look at the real thing—the flower you wish to duplicate—and copying the parts you see. Looking at a good photograph or botanical illustration will sometimes work, but there may be pitfalls in trying to determine sizes and shapes of parts that are not visible. In any case, examine the various flower parts, looking for similarities between this flower and flowers that you already know how to make. Next, trace the actual flower parts onto a piece of paper. Remember to make any minor adjustments in the pattern to ensure that you will be able to assemble it with floral tape and glue.

Another method of making your own patterns is to examine a commercially made silk flower and notice how it is formed. Take notes on color and number of petals and other flower parts. Then take it apart and adapt it to paper patterns that you can use. Some ready-made silk flowers have plastic parts, and you will have to duplicate them with fabric or floral tape to guarantee the quality of your flower.

An inexpensive way to test your new pattern is to create a prototype in crepe paper instead of silk. This will allow you to make adjustments to the pattern and refine your finished flower to your liking.

Once you have your pattern

2-2. Apply starch to the fabric with a brush (or a clean rag).

with sizing, allow it to dry in the open air. If you are in a hurry, a warm oven will dry it in three or four minutes. Before placing the material in the oven, however, warm it up for a few minutes at about 250° F, then turn it off. Overheating of some fabrics, particularly silk, will yellow and discolor them, so be sure not to put silk in the oven if the heat is turned on.

traced, whether an original or one taken from this book, the next step is to cut it out. This is a straightforward procedure, but be careful to cut ever so slightly inside your pencil marks on the fabric so that they will not show up on your finished flower. And remember to check, before cutting, that the arrow on the pattern is aligned with the grain on the fabric.

tablespoon of water. Stir mixture into one cup of boiling water. Heat and stir until the mixture is thickened. Then add one tablespoon of Sobo or white glue and stir. This mixture can be stored in your refrigerator for as long as two weeks.

After the fabric is saturated

Dyeing

After you have starched your fabric, you are ready to dye it. Dyeing is an important step toward adding beauty and creativity to your flowermaking efforts. You can use a variety of dyes; do not be afraid to experiment. Look in craft stores for dyes used for painting on fabric. Powdered dyes are generally the least expensive and give good results. (Chapter 1 has a list of some of the more successful dyes.)

Sizing

If the directions for the flower you have selected call for starched fabric, pick out the pieces of fabric you will be using. A one-foot-square piece is a good, workable size. You will need about one pint of sizing for each yard of material. Place the fabric on top of an old towel or cloth rag. Apply sizing with a brush or a rag (fig. 2-2). Wipe off the excess starch with a clean rag (fig. 2-3).

Here is a recipe that works very well for starching silk, cotton, and velvet. Mix one tablespoon of cornstarch with one

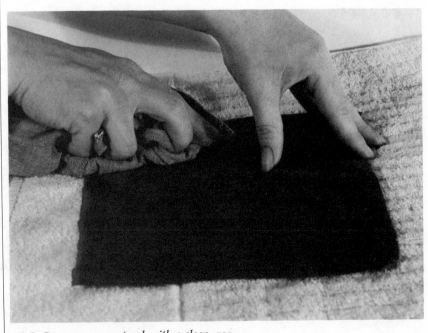

2-3. Remove excess starch with a clean rag.

2-4. Apply dye with a brush.

Experimenting with color is an exciting aspect of flower-making. With just the basic primary colors—red, blue, and yellow—you can create almost any color needed. You can make various shades of green by mixing proportionate amounts of blue and yellow, you can make orange by mixing red and yellow, and you can create brown out of your green and orange mixtures. You can make pastels by diluting the strong shades with water. You can obtain a beautiful dusty rose color by carefully mixing pink and brown. A few drops of a complementary color will deepen a tint—add a drop of blue to orange, yellow to purple, or green to red. You can obtain almost any secondary color by mixing.

To apply dye to petals and leaves, you will need the following materials: blotting paper (coarse newsprint will do), watercolor brushes, small bowls, dyes, water, and tweezers. Set a petal on the blotting paper and, with the brush, thoroughly wet it with water. Work out any bubbles by stroking outward toward the edges of the petal with the brush. Next apply dye to the desired area with a brush (fig. 2-4).

The dye will travel outward by capillary action, producing an interesting effect. This allows you to leave certain areas of the petal white. For example, a sweet pea may have just the edges dyed while the heart of the petal remains white. The petal of a gladiolus might have the center dyed, with the outer edges left pale or white. (See fig. 2-5.) You can also work with a deep color and a more diluted shade of the same color. For example, the morning glory petal should be dyed along its top edge with diluted dye, then the very tip of the edge should be dyed with a deeper hue of the same color; the base of the petal remains white.

You can dye leaves with diluted green, then deepen the centers with undiluted green. Tips or bases of a few leaves can be accented with a stroke of the dye used for the petal color.

Throughout the dyeing procedure, you may need to brush more water onto the petal or leaf to help the dye spread evenly. After the petals or leaves have been dyed, pick them up with tweezers and dry them on fresh blotting paper.

Gluing the Wire

Most petals and leaves need to be supported with wire, which must be covered with cloth that is the same color as the petal or leaf. If you cannot find the right color of cloth-covered wire in the craft store, buy white cloth-covered wire and use a brush to dye it the same color as the flower. Be

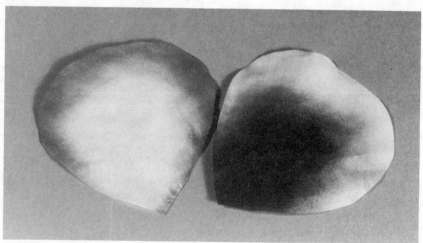

2-5. Sweet pea (left) and gladiolus petals.

sure it is thoroughly dry before gluing it to the petal or leaf.

The length of wire used varies with the size of the leaf or petal. Generally, it should reach almost to the tip and extend about 2 or 3 inches below the base of the petal or leaf.

To attach wire to a petal or leaf, apply glue with a toothpick along the length of the wire (fig. 2-6) and press the wire against the side of the fabric specified in the instructions. Sometimes the instructions for a particular flower will specify that two petals be placed back to back with glue between them. In this case, glue must be placed along two opposite sides of the cloth-covered wire so that both petals are glued together only at the wire. Always apply glue to the wire, rather than the silk, unless the instructions specify otherwise.

Shaping Flower Parts

Petals and other flower parts are shaped by using heated tools. The tool you use will determine the shape you obtain. You can purchase specialized Japanese tools or improvise with a variety of household tools, but at least two dinner knives without serrated edges are essential. Bind the blade of one of them and the handle of the other with cloth or hot pads (figs. 2-7 and 2-8). (The unbound ends will be placed at the heat source.) The heated knife edge is used to make the veins of leaves, and the heated knife handle is used to curve petals and other parts of the flowers. We have also used nut picks, forks, and spoons to good effect.

There are a number of safe ways to heat your tools. The best is to use an electric hot plate,

2-6. *Apply a small amount of glue to the wire with a toothpick.*

over which you have placed wire mesh. The wire mesh should be able to withstand high temperatures when it is placed about an inch above the electric heating coils. The tools then can sit on top of the mesh, with their handles resting on a block of wood

2-7. *Wrap dinner-knife blade with cloth.*

2-8. *Wrap dinner-knife handle with cloth.*

beside the hot plate. (See fig. 2-9.) If your tools do not have wooden handles, or if you are using stainless ware, they will heat up over their entire length: handle them carefully with a thick hot pad or glove. You can also wrap a metal handle with a cloth rag and bind it securely.

You can also heat tools by placing them in boiling water (wipe dry before using) or by placing tools in a saucepan partially filled with fine-quality table salt that has been heated to about 250° F. Be sure to remove the pan from the heat while you are using the tools. The salt will retain the heat for a short period.

2-9. *Electric hot plate covered with wire mesh.*

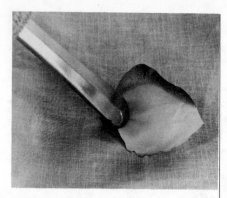

2-10. *Use the knife handle to iron a petal.*

To shape petals or to make veins in leaves, place the fabric pieces on heavy foam rubber that has been covered with white cotton fabric. Test your hot tools on a piece of scrap silk to make sure they will not burn your silk. Then press the heated tool on the places specified in the instructions. (See figs. 2-10 and 2-11.) The pressing locations are indicated by *X*s on the drawings of petals and calyxes. When the *X*s are made of dashed lines, you should iron the fabric on the opposite side with the heated knife handle. (See fig. 2-12.)

The instructions for ironing veins on leaves specify two vein types—simple branching and compound branching. Simple branching involves using the heated knife edge to make lines,

2-11. *Use the knife edge to iron veins of a leaf.*

on the wired side of a leaf, that branch directly outward from the central wire. Then you turn the leaf over onto its unwired side and use the knife edge to make the central crease right next to the wire. (See fig. 2-13.) Compound branching involves making more complex branching lines, on the wired side of a leaf, that branch outward from the central wire. You then turn the leaf over

2-12. *A solid X means iron here; a dashed-line X means iron on the opposite side of the fabric at that spot.*

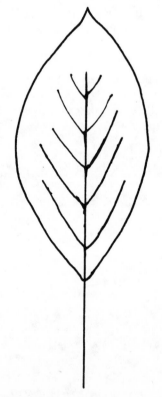

2-13. *Simple branching veins.*

onto its unwired side and make the central crease with your heated knife edge right next to the wire. (See fig. 2-14.)

Making Stamens

Commercial stamens work well with handmade flowers, but to achieve an even more handmade effect, you might wish to make your stamens from wire, baker's clay, glue, and acrylic paint.

To make the dough for baker's clay, mix two tablespoons of flour, one tablespoon of salt, and one tablespoon of water. Cut some cloth-covered wire (#30) into lengths of 3 inches or more and add a small amount of glue to the tips of each of the pieces of wire. Mold dough to the desired shape around the tips of the wires. Bake in a moderate oven (350° F) for about ten minutes, or until they are slightly brown. Paint them the desired color with

2-14. *Compound branching veins.*

acrylic paint, or leave them toasty brown. You can also make stamens by wrapping narrow strips of floral tape around tips of cloth-covered wire. (A number of the flower projects in this book have stamens that are made this way.)

Making Buds and Tendrils

It is easy to make many types of buds with absorbent cotton and wire. Apply a small amount of glue to the tip of the stem wire. Take small pieces of absorbent cotton and wrap them around the tip of the stem wire. Keep adding more pieces of cotton and wrap until you have created a cocoon shape (some buds require even smaller amounts of cotton). Then add silk or other fabrics according to the specific instructions.

Tendrils add a delicate flair to some flowers. Wrap green cloth-covered wire (#30) spirally along the length of an awl, starting at the awl's point. Apply the tendril to the stem just as you would apply a leaf—by wrapping with green floral tape.

Assembly

To create a flower from its petals, you must first cluster the stamens. Apply glue to the tip of stem wire and wrap together the stem and the stamens with floral tape. As you pull this tape it becomes sticky, so remember to stretch the tape as you wrap. Wrap only about ½ inch. Next place the base of the petals around the base of the stamens, usually with the unwired side facing inward. Wrap to secure them with no petal stem wire showing below the base of the petal. If instructions call for a calyx, apply a small amount of glue at the base of the calyx and wrap it below the petals. Wrap the stem with floral tape, add leaves (usually with no leaf stem wire showing), wrap with more floral tape, and attach more leaves until you have achieved the desired effect. Buds and tendrils can be added along the way as you wrap with floral tape to the end of the main stem wire. Figures 2-15 through 2-19 show the assembly process of a sweet pea. (See

Chapter 20 for patterns and more details.)

Instead of using floral tape, you might wish to use thin strips of fabric dyed to the desired color. Apply glue a short distance along the stem wire and turn the stem wire, wrapping the strip downward spirally and applying more glue along the wire as needed

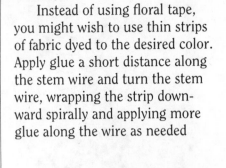

2-17. Add another bud, a leaf, and a tendril.

2-15. Sweet pea assembly, starting with a bud.

2-16. Add a flower and a leaf.

2-18. Wrap the floral tape in a downward direction.

2-19. Add the final flower.

(fig. 2-20). This technique gives a more handmade look and is especially appropriate for flowers such as poppies and anemones when velvet strips are used to wrap the stems.

Special Effects

Special effects, such as rolled or waved edges, make a silk flower unique and lifelike. This section details several techniques that will give your handmade flowers authentic looks.

Rolled-edge Silk Flowers

Making rolled-edge silk flowers is a special technique that requires a bit of practice before mastery, but once it is perfected, it will add unbelievable elegance and a fine handmade touch to your flowers. With this method it is possible to create silk flowers that are truly poetic.

Not all the flower patterns in this book can be used for rolled-edge flowers. Some small petals may have to be specially adapted by tracing the pattern so that it will come out slightly larger. There is no way that you can use this technique on tiny petals, such as those of lilacs or geraniums. Medium-to-large petals are easy to roll. Leaves generally do not have rolled edges. To make the leaves for rolled-edge flowers, use the same techniques for cutting, sizing, and dyeing as previously described.

The first step in making rolled-edge flowers is selecting the fabric. Once again, 100 percent China silk works best. Other silks that are partly synthetic, such as crepe de chine and silk charmeuse, may also be used, because starching is not necessary for rolled-edge silk flowers. The important consideration in fabric selection is to determine whether or not the edges will "roll." Take a container of Sobo glue to the fabric store and ask for a small sample of the fabric that you are considering buying. If the edges will roll easily, according to the instructions that follow, then the fabric will suit your needs. Remember, however, that if you wish to dye the rolled-edge flowers, you are safest in selecting China silk—the others do not accept dyes as well. (Dye the fabric according to the instructions given earlier in this chapter. After the petals are dry, you can roll their edges.)

To start the edge-rolling process, first squeeze a small puddle of Sobo glue onto a piece of scrap paper. With a toothpick, apply very small amounts of glue to the edge of the petal you intend to roll. Hold about 1 inch of the petal with your left hand and carefully grasp the glued edge between the thumb and forefinger of your right hand and roll the edge (fig. 2-21). Add more glue to the adjacent edge and continue rolling this way until you have rolled all edges of the petal. The petal will be sculptured and have lovely waves and ripples along the edges (fig. 2-22). While you are rolling the petal, it is important to keep a damp rag on your lap at all times to wipe glue off your fingers. Once glue is smeared on a petal, there is nothing you can do to remove it. Practice on a few small scrap pieces of silk before you attempt to roll a petal. And be sure to persevere—it is well worth the effort.

Rolled-edge petals may be wired with cloth-covered wire

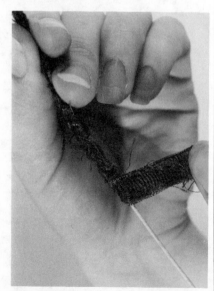

2-20. Fabric-wrapped stem.

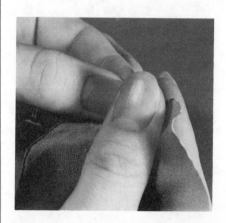

2-21. Roll the glued edge of the petal.

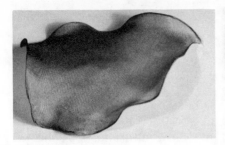

2-22. *Finished rolled-edge petal.*

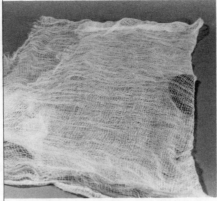

2-23. *Fold a petal into a piece of cheese-cloth.*

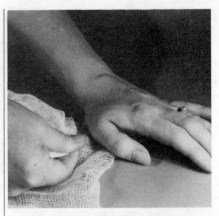

2-24. *Hold the cheesecloth and the petal down with one hand and pull across and around with the other hand.*

(#30). These flowers are assembled just as other flowers are; simply follow the instructions for the assembly of the particular flower you are making.

Wrinkling Petals

This technique gives a professional quality to your handmade flowers. You can use the method for regular cut-edge flowers that are made from starched silk or you can use it with rolled-edge flowers that are not starched. For rolled-edge petals, roll the edges first before you wrinkle the petals. The technique is easy and requires no hot tools—it works best for flowers such as the iris, anemone, Oriental poppy, and hibiscus.

Take your wired flower petal and wet it very lightly with a mister. Fold the petal in half along the wire and place it inside a folded piece of cheesecloth. Make sure that the folded edges of the petal and the cheesecloth are together, toward the right side, and the wire extends downward (fig. 2-23). Now place the fleshy part of your hand directly on the petal and press firmly. With your other hand, pull the top right edge of the cheesecloth almost all the way around in a counter-clockwise direction (fig. 2-24). Be sure to pull firmly, almost to the point of tearing the cheesecloth. Remove and unfold the petal. You will see lovely symmetrical waves

and ripples all along the petal (fig. 2-25).

Waving Edges

This method works best after you have wrinkled the petals with cheesecloth. Place your thumbs and forefingers together along the edge of a wrinkled petal (fig. 2-26). Pull forward and back, as if you were planning to tear the fabric. (Silk is strong and will not tear if you wave the edges carefully.) Repeat this process until the entire edge of the petal is crinkled and looks wavy.

The Reality Factor

You can do a number of

things to make your flowers more realistic. When dyeing, for example, select appropriate colors. You can achieve an interesting mottled effect with some dyes by sprinkling fine grains of salt on leaves and petals while dyeing. For fall arrangements, dye leaves autumn colors—browns, oranges, yellows, and reds. Or dye leaves green with some brown areas so that they look as though they are just turning brown. A sprig of brown, mottled, bladelike leaves adds an interesting touch to a collection of fall flowers.

You can create spotted leaves

2-25. *Finished wrinkled petal.*

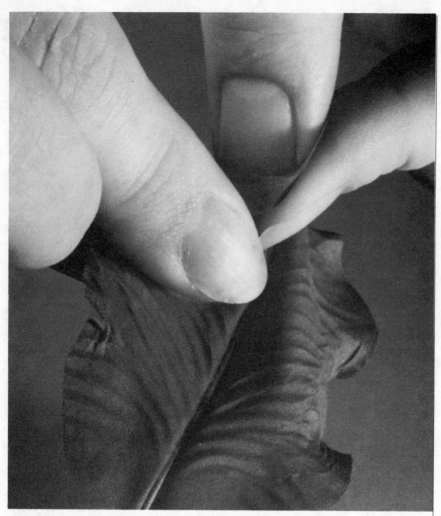

2-26. *Pull the petal in opposite directions to wave the edges.*

and petals and specks of pollen grains by making dots with colored markers. And you can enhance the vein patterns of leaves by tracing over them with colored markers.

Scenting is a fine extra touch of reality, but it must be done very carefully. Scented oils can stain fabric easily and create ugly, greasy-looking spots if they are not used properly. To scent a rose, for example, start by wrapping the tip of the stem wire with thin strips of tissue paper and glue. Wrap down only 1 inch. Dip about ¼ inch of this end in rose-scented oil (available in some craft stores or cosmetics stores). Then wrap the oil-soaked tissue with a small amount of absorbent cotton and assemble the flower according to the instructions.

If you wish to be even more reaslistic, you can cut small indentations in the edges of leaves to create an insect-eaten look.

Once you experience the pleasure of creating your own silk flowers, you will be surprised at how often you will notice, appreciate, and want to duplicate the beauty of the real thing.

· PART II ·
THE
FLOWERS

CHAPTER 3

CARNATION

The carnation, sometimes called the gillyflower, is in the genus *Dianthus,* of which there are a great many hybrids. In Victorian flower language, the carnation signifies fascination. A yellow carnation can mean disdain; a striped one, refusal.

Materials
silk: white
cotton (optional)
dyes: yellowish green, green, pink
green cloth-covered wire: #30
floral tape: green, yellow
stem wire: #16, #18
absorbent cotton

Assembly
1 flower
2 buds
3 calyxes
6 leaves

Following the patterns given here (figs. 3-2 through 3-6), cut four large petals and two bud petals out of white silk. Cut one large calyx, two bud calyxes, and six leaves out of silk or the optional cotton.

Dye the center of each petal circle yellowish green. Dye the circumference of each petal circle pink or leave it white. Dye the leaves and calyxes green.

3-1. *Carnation.*

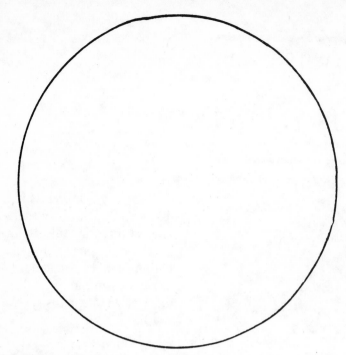

3-2. *Flower petal.*

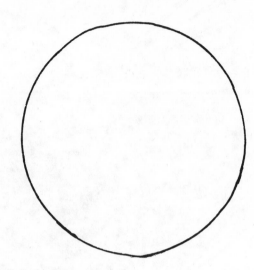

3-3. *Bud petal.*

Glue green cloth-covered wire along the center of each leaf, allowing 2 inches of the wire to extend below the base of the leaf.

Fold a petal in half to form a semicircle. With small, sharp scissors, snip the edges, giving the effect of butterfly wings (fig. 3-7). Unfold the petal. Do this to all petals, including the bud petals.

Iron each petal with a heated knife handle, following the *X*s in figure 3-8.

Take a 12-inch length of #16 stem wire and wrap yellow floral tape around one end to form a small knob about ⅛ inch in diameter. Take two 6-inch lengths of #18 stem wire and do

the same to their tips. These two shorter wires will be used for the buds.

Pierce the center of a large petal circle with an awl on the ironed side and apply glue around the hole on the ironed side. Slip the #16 wire through the hole on the ironed side and slide the petal circle up near the yellow knob. Pinch the petal circle on the underside below the knob. Follow the same procedure with the three other petal circles, sliding them up below the others and pinching them at the base. Wrap with absorbent cotton right below the flower to form a 1-inch cocoon shape (fig. 3-9). Apply glue to the base of a large calyx and wrap it around the absorbent

cotton, pinching the calyx at the base. Wrap below the calyx and down the wire a few inches with green floral tape. Wrap on two leaves near each other about 2 inches below the flower.

To make the two buds, pierce the center of each petal circle with an awl on the ironed side. Apply glue near the hole of one petal on the ironed side and slide it up and under the yellow knob at the tip of one of the #18 stem

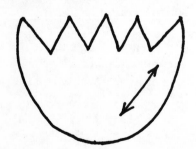

3-4. *Flower calyx.*

3-5. *Bud calyx.*

3-6. *Leaf.*

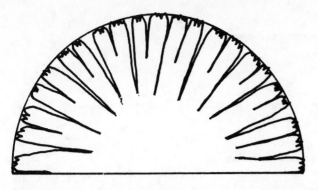

3-7. *Cut the petals from the folded petal circle.*

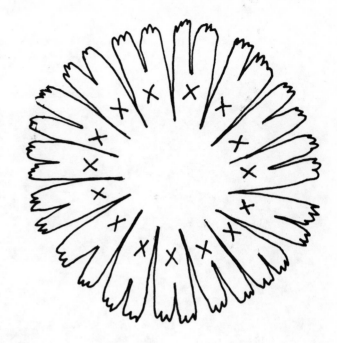

3-8. *Iron each petal at the Xs.*

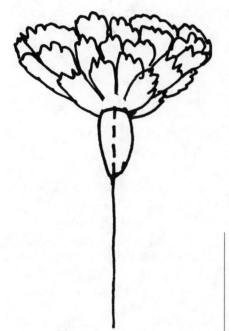

3-9. *Wrap absorbent cotton around the base of the flower.*

wires. Pinch it tightly at its base. Wrap below the bud with absorbent cotton and attach the calyx just as you did for the flower. Wrap below the calyx and down the stem with green floral tape. Make one more bud the same way.

To assemble the finished flower, continue wrapping below the flower with green floral tape. Add a bud, then two leaves, as you wrap. Continue this way, adding the other bud and two leaves as you wrap to the end of the stem wire with the tape.

CHAPTER 4

NASTURTIUM

*T*he nasturtium (in the family Tropaeolaceae) is a perennial that tends to climb. It generally flowers in red or orange, and many of its species are edible. If you have ever eaten watercress, for example, you've tasted a close relative of this flower. Linnaeus named this flower family—from the Greek word *troparion,* meaning trophy.

Materials
silk: white
dyes: yellow, orange (optional), green
marker: red or burgundy
orange or yellow cloth-covered wire: #30
green cloth-covered wire: #30
commercial stamen: yellow
stem wire: #18
thin strips of tissue paper
floral tape: green

Assembly
1 flower
1 bud
3 leaves
2 calyxes

Following the patterns given here (figs. 4-2 through 4-7), cut five petals out of silk. Cut one of each of the three sizes of leaves,

4-1. Nasturtium.

4-2. *Flower petal.*

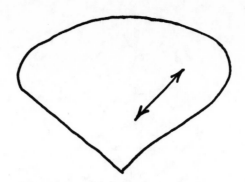

4-3. *Bud petal.*

4-4. *Calyx.*

one bud, and two calyxes—all out of silk.

Dye the petals and the bud orange or yellow. Dye the calyx yellow and the leaves green. When the petals are dry, use a red or burgundy marker to make a few streaks extending up and outward near the base of two of the petals. Make the lines as fine as you can—heavy lines destroy the natural look.

Glue orange or yellow cloth-covered wire (depending on which color you dyed the petals) along the center of each petal, allowing about 2 inches of the wire to extend below the base of the petal. The leaves are wired differently. Glue green cloth-covered wire along only half the width of the leaf, then bend it to make it look as though the stem is emerging from the center of the leaf. Then glue a short length of wire in a wide, upside-down V shape below the first wire. This will help hold the leaf outward and prevent its sides from flopping over. (See fig. 4-8.)

Iron each leaf with a heated knife edge on the wired side (fig. 4-9). Iron each petal with a heated knife handle on the wired side as shown by the *X*s in figure 4-10.

Bend six or eight of the commercial stamen in half (fig. 4-11A). Secure them to the tip of a 12-inch length of #18 stem wire by wrapping the base of the stamen with thin strips of tissue paper and glue (fig. 4-11B). Now take the two petals with streaks and place them together near the base of the stamen, with unwired sides showing. Arrange the other three petals around the stamen, with the unwired sides showing. Secure these petals to the stem wire just below the stamen by wrapping all the wires with thin strips of tissue paper and glue. Wrap over the tissue paper with green floral tape for about three inches.

The calyx must be attached very carefully. Apply a small amount of glue only at the sides right below each side sepal; use the dashed lines in figure 4-12 as

4-5. *Large leaf.*

4-6. *Medium leaf.*

4-7. *Small leaf.*

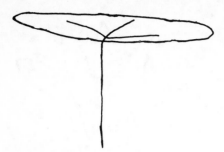

4-8. *V-shaped wire holds the broad leaf upright.*

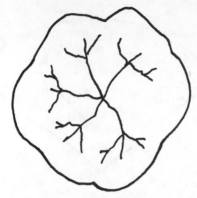

4-9. *Iron each leaf outward from the center.*

4-10. *Iron each petal at the Xs.*

a guide. Then wrap the calyx around the base of the flower. Bend the stem wire downward just below the flower so the pointed end of the calyx is perpendicular to the stem (fig. 4-13).

To make the bud, take a 5-inch length of stem wire #18 and apply a small amount of glue to its tip. Place the base (the point) of the bud fabric below the glued tip of the stem wire and roll the bud into a trumpet shape. Wrap below this (about 3 inches) with green floral tape. Attach the calyx

just below the bud in the same manner as for the flower and bend the stem wire at a right angle below the bud to make the pointed end of the calyx protrude.

The stems of the leaves must be wrapped carefully with thin strips of green floral tape before applying them to the flower stem. If cloth-covered wire shows as a leaf stem, it detracts from the appearance of the entire arrangement. Therefore, cut a strip of

green floral tape in half lengthwise. Use these strips to wrap around each leaf stem, thus eliminating bulkiness.

Now the flower is ready to be assembled. Continue wrapping down the flower stem with green floral tape. Add the bud and then the small leaf. Wrap farther down the stem with the floral tape and add the medium leaf and then the large one. Continue wrapping the stem with the tape to the end.

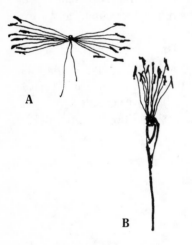

4-11. (A) *Wrap wire at the stamen centers and bend upward.* (B) *Wrap and glue tissue paper at the stamen base.*

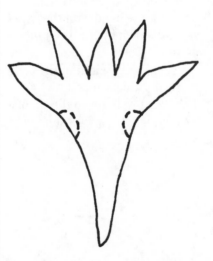

4-12. *Apply glue in areas within dashed lines on the sides of the calyx.*

4-13. *Bend the calyx so it is horizontal.*

CHAPTER 5

PANSY

*T*he pansy (in the family Viola-ceae) has long been associated with the Holy Trinity. The three central petals were said to represent the Father, the Son, and the Holy Ghost, with the dark center of the flower being the eye of God. In Britain the pansy once went by the name of herb trinity. In flower language the pansy can mean thoughtfulness or you occupy my thoughts.

Materials
silk: white, green (optional)
cotton (optional)
starch
dyes: burgundy, purple, blue, or
    yellow, plus black and green
cloth-covered wire to match the
    petals: #30
green cloth-covered wire: #30
stem wire: #18
floral tape: yellow, green

Assembly
1 flower
3 leaves
1 calyx

Following the patterns given here (figs. 5-2 through 5-4), cut five petals out of starched white silk. Cut three leaves and one calyx out of starched white or green silk or cotton.

5-1. *Pansy.*

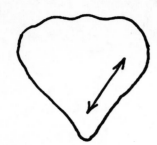

5-2. *Petal.*

5-3. *Calyx.*

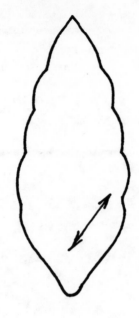

5-4. *Leaf.*

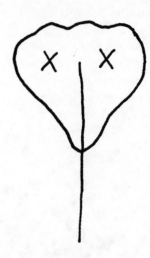

5-5. *Iron each petal at the Xs.*

Dye the petals burgundy, purple, blue, or yellow. Dye the bases of three petals black. This should be a deep black, not a dirty-looking, smudgy black. In order to achieve a rich black color, you might try experimenting by mixing some simple, inexpensive watercolors. Deepen the color with a few extra dabs with the brush. Dye the leaves and the calyx green.

Glue cloth-covered wire along the center of each petal with 2 inches extending below the base. Check both sides of the petal and

glue the wire to the side that did not absorb the black dye as readily. This will ensure that the side with the deeper black will be visible.

Glue green cloth-covered wire along the center of each leaf, allowing about 2 inches of the wire to extend below the base of the leaf.

Iron the leaves on the wired side with a heated knife edge, creating a simple branching vein structure. Iron the petals with a heated knife handle on the wired side, as shown by the *X*s in figure

5-5. Iron the calyx with a heated knife handle, as shown by the *X*s in figure 5-6.

To make a yellow center for the flower, take a 10-inch piece of

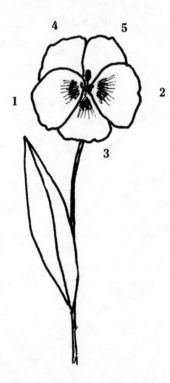

5-8. *Apply petals in the sequence indicated.*

5-6. *Iron the calyx at the Xs.*

5-7. *Make the stamens with stem wire and yellow floral tape.*

#18 stem wire and wrap its tip with a small piece of yellow floral tape so that it forms a small knob (fig. 5-7).

Now arrange the petals around the flower center. Start with the three blackened petals. Place one on each side of the yellow center and one below it.

Place the two plain petals close together at the top. (See fig. 5-8.) Wrap the petal stems to the stem wire with green floral tape and cut the tape right below the flower.

Before wrapping down the stem wire with floral tape, apply glue to the base of a calyx and wrap it around the stem wire just below the flower. Now wrap below the calyx and down the stem wire with green floral tape. Add the three leaves as you wrap to the end of the stem with floral tape. Give the flower a slight upward tilt from its base to make it more visible.

CHAPTER 6

HIBISCUS

*T*he hibiscus (in the family Malvaceae) has been culti-vated since earliest history in China. Sometimes colloquially called mallow or rose mallow, its blossoms are short-lived but very abundant. The hibiscus was named by Linnaeus, who may have related it to the ibis, a bird that is thought to have fed on some hibiscus varieties.

Materials
silk: white
cotton (optional)
dyes: pink or red, yellow or
    orange, green
cloth-covered wire to match the
    petals: #30
yellow cloth-covered wire: #30
green cloth-covered wire: #30
stem wire: #16
floral tape: yellow, green
thin strips of tissue paper

Assembly
1 flower
1 partially opened flower
5 small leaves
3 large leaves
2 calyxes
silk stamen strip

    Following the patterns given here (figs. 6-2 through 6-7), cut five large petals and ten small petals out of white silk. Dye them

6-1. *Hibiscus.*

26

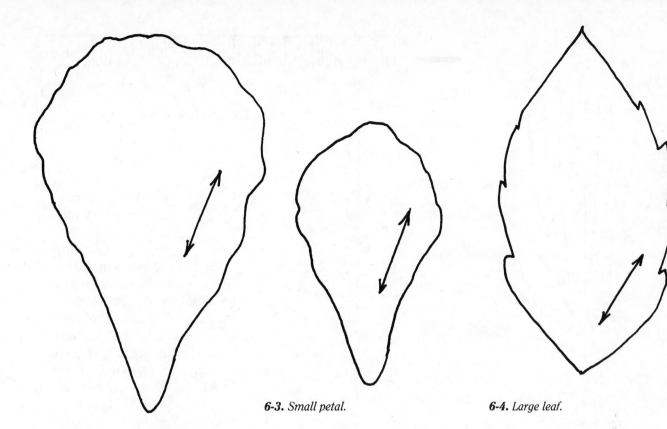

6-2. *Large petal.*

6-3. *Small petal.*

6-4. *Large leaf.*

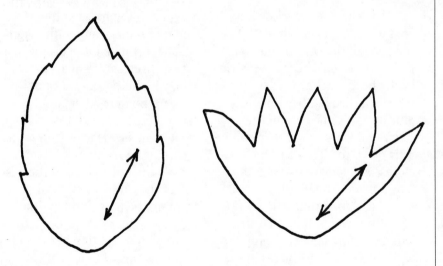

6-5. *Small leaf.*

6-6. *Calyx.*

pale pink or red. (Another technique is to cut petals out of yellow silk and dye the centers and the bases of the petals orange.) Cut one stamen strip out of silk and dye it yellow. (The stamen strip does not have to be cut on the bias.) Cut five small leaves and three large ones out of silk or cotton and dye them green. To make it easier to cut the leaves, trace them and cut them first in an oval shape. Then cut small notches along the sides to give the leaves a serrated edge. Cut two calyxes out of silk or cotton and dye them green.

Glue cloth-covered wire along the center of each petal, allowing 2 inches of the wire to extend

6-7. *Stamen strip.*

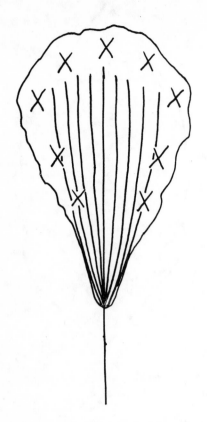

6-8. *Iron the large petal at the Xs and along vein lines on the wired side.*

6-10. *Wrap the stamen strip on the cloth-covered wire in a descending spiral.*

6-9. *Cut slits in the stamen strip and hook doubled wire onto the right edge of the strip.*

below the base. Use wire that matches the dyed petals. Iron the petals with a heated knife handle on the wired side, as shown by the *X*s in figure 6-8. Then iron the petals with a heated knife edge, showing simple radiating lines on the wired side.

Another method of shaping the petals is to wrinkle them with cheesecloth, then wave the edges. For details on this technique, see "Wrinkling Petals" and "Waving Edges" in Chapter 2.

Glue green cloth-covered wire along the center of each leaf, allowing 2 inches of wire to extend below the leaf base. With a heated knife edge, iron a compound vein structure on the wired side of the leaves.

To make the stamen, cut small slits along the top edge of the stamen strip. Then take a 10-inch length of yellow cloth-covered wire and bend it in half. Slip the bend of the wire through a slit at the end of the stamen strip so the bend catches the last slit of the strip. (See fig. 6-9.) Apply glue all along the base of the strip. Roll the stamen strip spirally down the doubled yellow cloth-covered wire to a length of 2 or 3 inches (fig. 6-10).

Attach the stamen to the tip of a 12-inch length of #16 stem wire by gluing and wrapping it with thin strips of white tissue paper. Then wrap over this tissue with yellow floral tape. Apply a small amount of glue to the unwired sides at the bases of five of the small petals and secure them below the stamen with unwired sides inward. Then position five large petals right below the small petals, with unwired

sides facing the stamen. Secure these petals by gluing and wrapping the stem wire right below the petals with thin strips of tissue paper and glue. Apply a small amount of glue to the base of a calyx and wrap it around the base of the flower. Wrap right below this with green floral tape for about 2 inches.

To make the partially opened flower, take a 5-inch length of #16 stem wire and wrap the tip for about 2 inches with yellow floral tape. Apply a small amount of glue to the bases of the wired sides of the remaining five small petals. Arrange them around the stem wire about 1 inch below the tip, with wired sides inward. Secure them by wrapping the stem wire for about 1 inch right below the petals with thin strips of tissue paper and glue. Apply a small amount of glue to the base of a calyx and wrap the calyx around the base of the partially opened flower. Wrap the stem wire with green floral tape and add two small leaves while you wrap.

To assemble the completed flower, finish wrapping the flower stem wire with green floral tape, adding three small leaves, then two large leaves, then the partially opened flower and the last large leaf. Wrap to the end of the stem wire with the tape.

CHAPTER 7

ROSE

*T*he rose (in the family Rosa-ceae) is perhaps the most romantic of flowers. Its scent is mysterious and intoxicating. In flower language the rose has a multitude of meanings, depending on the color and variety. A red rose can mean love or beauty; a white rose means silence. Red and white roses together mean warmth of heart.

Materials
silk: white
cotton or velvet (optional)
dyes: green, plus any rose color
green cloth-covered wire: #30
absorbent cotton
stem wire: #16, #18
green floral tape

Assembly
1 large rose
1 bud
2 sets of leaves
2 calyxes

Following the patterns given here (figs. 7-2 through 7-7), cut four large petals, four medium petals, and eight small petals out of silk. Cut two calyxes out of silk or cotton. Cut one large leaf and four small leaves out of silk or cotton. If you can find a variety of velvet that is receptive to sizing

7-1. Rose.

29

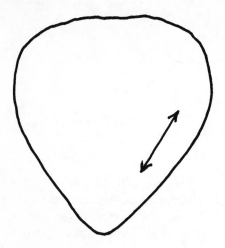

7-2. *Large petal.*

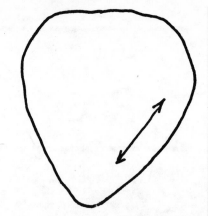

7-3. *Medium petal.*

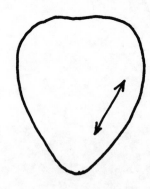

7-4. *Small petal.*

and dyes, it works well for making leaves and calyxes.

Dye the petals any desired color. You can achieve a very fine look by first dyeing the base of each petal yellowish green, then dyeing the rest of the petal another color. To make an elegant white rose, leave it white with a yellowish-green base on each petal. Dye the leaves and calyxes green.

Glue green cloth-covered wire along the center of the leaves, allowing about 2 inches of the wire to extend below the base. With a heated knife edge, make veins on the leaves on the wired side, showing a simple branching vein structure.

Press the petals with a heated knife handle, as shown by the *X*s

in figure 7-8. Also press the sepals of the calyx with a heated knife handle, as shown by the *X*s in figure 7-9.

To start the flower, wrap absorbent cotton around the tip of a 12-inch length of #16 stem wire. Keep adding more cotton until you have a small cocoon shape. Cover three-fourths of the surface of one of the small petals with glue on the ironed side, starting at the base. Wrap the petal snugly around the absorbent cotton so that no cotton shows at the tip. Some cotton may show at the base, but this will be covered up by more petals. Now place

glue on about half of the ironed surface of another small petal and wrap it around the first petal so that no cotton shows. Apply glue only to the base on the unironed sides of three more small petals and arrange these alternately around the first two petals, as shown in figure 7-10. (The glue is applied to the *unironed* sides of these three small petals so that when they are placed around the stem, they curve outward.)

Next add the four medium petals. Place a small amount of glue at the base of each one on the unironed side. Place these petals alternately around the small petals and be sure they curve outward. Follow the same

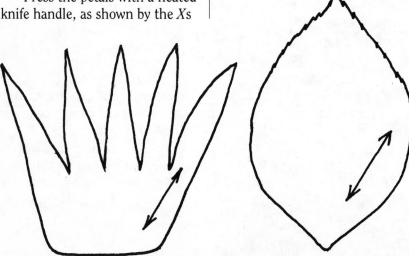

7-5. *Calyx.*

7-6. *Large leaf.*

7-7. *Small leaf.*

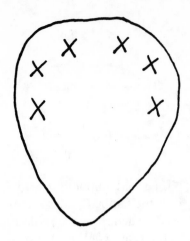

7-8. *Iron each petal at the Xs.*

7-9. *Iron the sepals of the calyx at the Xs.*

7-10. *Surround the first two petals with three small petals.*

procedure with the four large petals.

Wrap the #16 stem wire with absorbent cotton below the flower so it bulges slightly. Then apply glue to the entire base of the calyx and wrap the calyx base completely around the absorbent cotton below the flower. This forms the rosehip and gives your flower that special handmade look. To make the rosehip really bulge out, take a 5-inch length of thin wire (green cloth-covered wire #30 will do) and wrap it once around the calyx right where the sepals emerge (fig. 7-11). Twist the wire tightly at the ends and leave it this way for twenty-four hours to let the glue

set. Untwist and remove the wire carefully the next day.

Group one large leaf and two small leaves so that the large leaf is in the center, with a small leaf at each side (fig. 7-12). Wrap their wires with green floral tape. You will use this set of leaves with the large flower.

Make another set of leaves the same way, but use only two small leaves together. Wrap their stems with green floral tape. You will use this set of leaves with the bud.

To assemble the completed large flower, wrap right below the calyx with green floral tape. Add

the set of three leaves while you wrap down to the end of the stem wire with the tape.

To make the bud, start with a 12-inch length of #18 stem wire. Wrap its tip with absorbent cotton to form a cocoon shape and add three small petals in the same manner as you did for the large flower, applying glue to the ironed side of each petal. Stop adding petals after the third small petal. Wrap below this with absorbent cotton, attach the calyx, and form the rosehip just as you did for the flower. Wrap the stem wire with green floral tape and add the set of two leaves as you wrap down to the end of the stem wire with floral tape.

Medium-Sized Rose

To make the medium-sized rose (also shown in figure 7-1), use the same patterns and instructions as for the rose, but do not cut any large petals. Cut three medium petals and five small petals. Arrange these as you do for the rose. Add the same size calyx and form the rosehip in just the same manner. You may use the same leaves (either the two- or three-leaf set will work) or cut them slightly smaller.

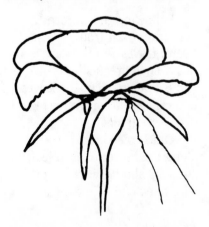

7-11. *Wrap #16 stem wire just below the sepals.*

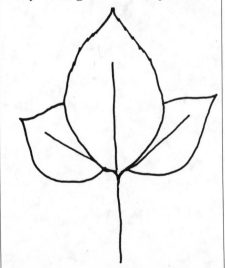

7-12. *Place one small leaf on each side of a large one.*

CHAPTER 8

SMALL CLIMBING ROSE

*T*he small climbing rose found in the family Rosaceae combines the delicacy of the wild rose and the beauty of the cultivated variety. In white this rose can signify silence or purity. In pink or red its flower meaning can be fidelity.

Materials

silk: white, green
starch
dye: green (optional)
green cloth-covered wire: #30
floral tape: green
stem wire: #16, #20
commercial stamen: yellow
thin strips of tissue paper
absorbent cotton

Assembly

5 flowers
12 leaves
2 buds (optional)

Following the patterns given here (figs. 8-2 through 8-4), cut twelve leaves and five calyxes out of starched green silk. If no green silk is available, cut the leaves and calyxes out of white silk and dye them green.

Glue green cloth-covered wire along the center of each leaf, allowing about 3 inches of the wire to extend below the base.

8-1. Small climbing rose.

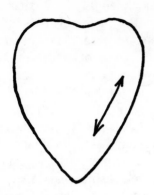

8-2. *Petal.*

8-3. *Calyx.*

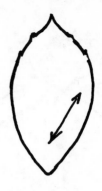

8-4. *Leaf.*

8-5. *Iron each petal at the Xs.*

8-6. *Iron the calyx at the Xs.*

8-7. *A two-leaf group.*

Iron each leaf on the wired side with a heated knife edge, showing a simple branching vein structure. Iron the petals and calyxes with a heated knife handle, as shown by the *X*s in figures 8-5 and 8-6.

Arrange the leaves in three different groups—a two-leaf set, a three-leaf set, and a seven-leaf set (figs. 8-7 through 8-9). Wrap their stems with green floral tape.

Make five stamen clusters. Take a 6-inch length of #20 stem wire. Gather about twelve yellow stamen and wrap the wire around the center of the stamen once and twist it tightly (fig. 8-10). Bend all the stamen upward. Wrap thin strips of tissue paper and glue around the base of the stamen cluster and down the wire (fig. 8-11).

8-8. *A three-leaf group.*

8-9. *A seven-leaf group.*

8-10. *Tie stamens at their centers with #20 stem wire.*

8-11. *Bend stamens upward and wrap with tissue paper.*

8-12. *Wrap the calyx with green cloth-covered wire just below the sepals.*

Apply glue to the base of six petals on the ironed side. Arrange the petals alternately around the stamen and wrap below the flower with absorbent cotton to form a small cocoon shape. Apply glue to the base of the calyx and wrap it around the absorbent cotton. Pinch the calyx at its base. Then take a short length of green cloth-covered wire, wrap it once right below the sepals, and twist tightly (fig. 8-12). This will form the rosehip. After about twenty-four hours, untwist and remove the wire carefully. Wrap below the calyx and down the stem with green floral tape.

To assemble the flowers, take a 12-inch length of #16 stem wire. Attach a flower to its tip by wrapping with green floral tape. Add the group of two leaves. Add more flowers, then the group of three leaves. Add the other flowers and the last group of seven leaves and wrap to the end of the stem wire with the floral tape.

If you wish to make a bud, cut three more petals and one calyx, using the patterns in figures 8-2 and 8-3. Follow the directions in Chapter 7 for making a regular rosebud. Incorporate the bud while assembling the flowers.

CHAPTER 9

DAFFODIL AND NARCISSUS

*T*he daffodil and the narcissus (both in the family Amaryllidaceae) are perennial bulbs with blossoms that vary in color from white to orange. In flower language the daffodil signifies regard or chivalry. The narcissus gets its name from the Greek word *narkan,* meaning to stupefy, because the flower was thought to possess narcotic powers. Some historians, however, related the name to the shepherd Narcissus, in Greek mythology, who fell in love with his own reflection. We have teamed these two flowers together in one chapter because they look alike and are made using similar techniques.

Materials for Daffodil or Narcissus
silk: white, yellow (optional)
cotton (optional)
dyes: yellow, green, yellowish
    brown, orange
yellow cloth-covered wire: #30
green cloth-covered wire: #30
thread: yellow
commercial stamens: white
stem wire: #16
thin strips of tissue paper
floral tape: green
marker: orange (optional)

9-1. Narcissus (left) and daffodil.

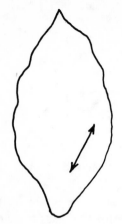

9-2. *Petal.*

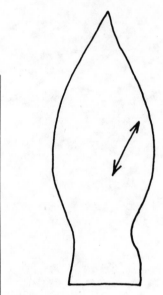

9-3. *Trumpet.*

Daffodil Assembly

1 flower
2 leaves
1 bract

Following the patterns given here (figs. 9-2 through 9-5), cut six petals and one trumpet out of white or yellow silk. Cut two leaves and one bract out of silk or cotton.

Dye the petals and trumpet yellow, and dye all the other pieces green, except for the bract, which can be yellowish brown for a more realistic look.

Glue yellow cloth-covered wire along the center of each petal, allowing about 2 inches of wire to extend below the base. Glue green cloth-covered wire along the center of each leaf, allowing about 2 inches to extend below the base.

Sometimes it is a good idea to glue two pieces of green cloth-covered wire side by side along the center of the leaf. This strengthens the long, bladelike leaf and keeps it from drooping. This is especially helpful if you are using a heavy fabric, such as cotton. You do not need to iron

9-4. *Bract.*

the leaf, but you may wish to make one long crease along the wire with a heated knife edge.

Iron each petal with a heated knife handle on the wired side, as shown by the *X*s in figure 9-6. Iron the bract with a heated knife edge, making about eight longitudinal creases.

Sew wide running stitches along the base of the trumpet (do not knot or finish off). Then moisten your fingertips and pinch all along the top edge to form wavy bulges. (See figure 9-7.) Iron the wavy edge with a heated knife handle, as shown by the *X*s in figure 9-8. This should make small crinkles along the edge of

9-5. *Leaf.*

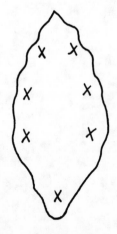

9-6. *Iron each petal at the Xs.*

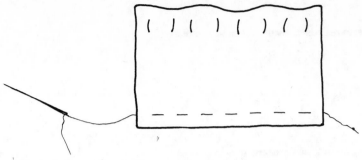

9-7. *Sew running stitches and wave the edges of the trumpet.*

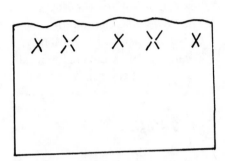

9-8. *Iron the trumpet at the Xs.*

9-9. *Wrap the stamens with tissue paper.*

the trumpet. Now use the heated knife edge to iron the trumpet longitudinally, making about eighteen creases. Next join the sides of the trumpet with a small amount of glue to form a cylinder. The running stitches should be at the base of the cylinder.

Cut off the ends of six to twelve commercial stamen. Attach them to the tip of a piece of #16 stem wire with thin strips of white tissue paper and glue. Wrap more strips of the tissue paper around this to form a slight bulge, the ovary. (See figure 9-9.)

Apply a small amount of glue along the inside base of the trumpet near the stitches. Insert the stem wire into the trumpet until the ovary is just above the stitches. Pull the thread until the base of the trumpet gathers around the base of the ovary.

Apply a small amount of glue to the unwired side of each petal near the base and attach the glued section to the base of the trumpet. Arrange the six petals so they surround the trumpet, wired sides down.

Wrap green floral tape around the stem wire just below the petals for about 2 inches. Apply a small amount of glue to the base of the bract on the ironed side and wrap it around the stem 2 inches below the flower. Below the bract, wrap floral tape along the stem. Attach the leaves as you wrap down to the end of the stem wire with floral tape. Where the bract emerges, bend the stem wire at about a forty-five-degree angle.

Narcissus Assembly

It is easy to adapt the instructions for the daffodil to create the narcissus (fig. 9-1). You follow the same instructions, except that the trumpet of the narcissus is about 1½ inches shorter than that of the daffodil. The trumpet width is the same. Because of the shorter trumpet, the stamen for narcissi are about half as long as daffodil stamen. The perianth (outer petals) of the narcissus may be white, while the trumpet is orange or yellow. This flower can also have a yellow perianth with an orange trumpet or a white trumpet with orange tips. You can use orange markers to color the tip of the trumpet.

CHAPTER 10

IRIS

*T*he iris (in the family Irida-ceae) was known in the ancient world and seems to have been cultivated by the Egyptians. The flower was named for Iris, Greek goddess of the rainbow, because its blossoms came in all the colors of the rainbow.

Materials

silk: white
cotton (optional)
dyes: purple or blue, yellowish
    green, green
white or yellow cloth-covered
    wire: #30
green cloth-covered wire: #30
3 chenille bumps: ivory or pale
    yellow
commercial stamen: yellow,
    white, or black
stem wire: #16
thin strips of tissue paper
floral tape: green

Assembly

1 flower
2 small leaves
1 large leaf

Following the patterns given here (figs. 10-2 through 10-4), cut six petals out of white silk. Cut two small leaves and one large leaf out of silk or cotton.

10-1. Iris.

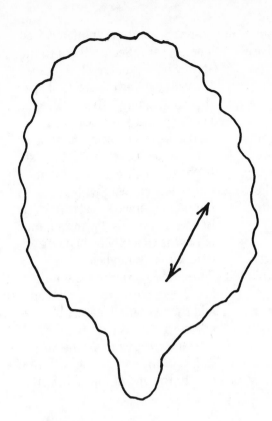

10-2. *Petal.*

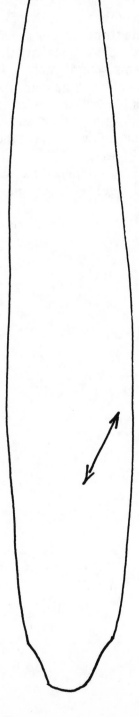

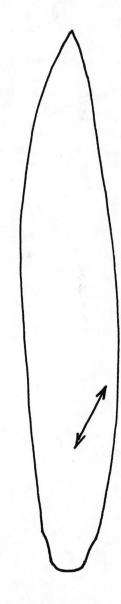

Dye the base of each petal yellowish green and the rest of the petal purple or blue. Deepen the color at the edges of the petals. Dye the leaves green.

Glue white or yellow cloth-covered wire along the center of the petals, allowing 2 inches of the wire to extend below the base. Glue green cloth-covered wire along the center of each leaf, allowing 2 inches of the wire to extend below the base.

Do not iron the petals with hot tools—use cheesecloth to wrinkle them and wave the edges. This gives a realistic look and adds a very professional touch. See "Wrinkling Petals" and "Waving Edges" in Chapter 2 for the details of this technique.

Cut the chenille bumps so they are about 3 inches long. Snip one side flat with scissors. Glue chenille bumps on only three petals. Apply glue to the flat side of a bump and place it along

10-3. *Large leaf.*

10-4. *Small leaf.*

10-5. *Glue chenille bump along center of a petal.*

the center of a petal, with about an inch extending below the base (fig. 10-5).

Iron each leaf with one lengthwise crease along the wire, using a heated knife edge.

Make a cluster of stamen at the tip of an 18-inch #16 stem wire. Cut the ends off about six stamens and attach them to the tip of the wire by wrapping with thin strips of tissue paper and glue. Since irises have thick stems, you may want to thicken the width of the stem. To do this, wrap down the stem repeatedly with strips of the tissue paper and glue until you achieve the desired thickness.

To assemble the flower, place the three petals without chenille pumps around the stamen, wired sides inward. Secure them to the stem wire with green floral tape. Curve the wires inward to shape the petals gently. These three petals should extend upward. Next take the three remaining petals and place them right next to the other three. Wrap them onto the stem wire with green floral tape, unwired sides inward. Bend these petals downward and curve them gently by bending their wires. Wrap below the flower and down the stem for a few inches with green floral tape. Add the two small leaves. Wrap a few more inches with the floral tape and then wrap on the large leaf. Continue wrapping with the tape to the end of the stem wire.

CHAPTER 11

GARDENIA

*T*he gardenia (of the family Rubiaceae) is an Oriental plant imported to the West some time after 1750. It grows in the form of an evergreen shrub and has particularly fragrant blossoms.

Materials
silk: white, green (optional)
dyes: green, yellowish green (both optional)
green cloth-covered wire: #30
stem wire: #16, #18
thin strips of tissue paper
floral tape: green

Assembly
1 large flower
1 partially opened flower
1 bud
5 large leaves
8 small leaves
3 calyxes

Following the patterns given here (figs. 11-2 through 11-6), cut five large petals and thirteen small petals out of white silk. Either leave them white, or for a natural touch, dye each of their bases yellowish green. Cut eight small leaves, five large leaves, and three calyxes out of green silk—or use white silk and dye them green.

11-1. Gardenia.

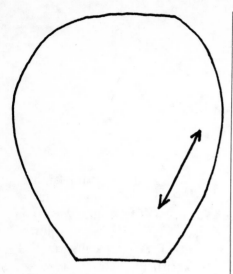

11-2. Large petal.

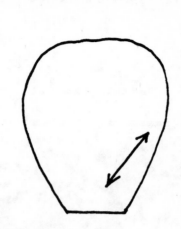

11-3. Small petal.

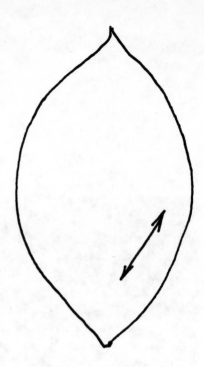

11-4. Large leaf.

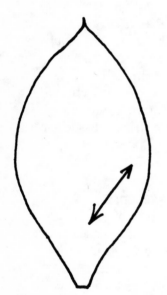

11-5. Small leaf.

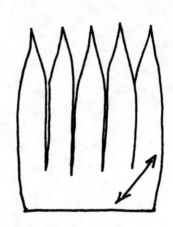

11-6. Calyx.

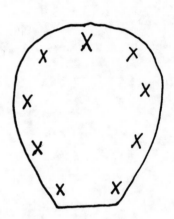

11-7. Iron each petal at the Xs.

Glue green cloth-covered wire along the center of each leaf, allowing 2 inches of the wire to extend below the base.

Iron each leaf with a heated knife edge to show a simple branching vein structure. Iron each petal with a heated knife handle, as shown by the *X*s in figure 11-7.

To make a bud, start with a 12-inch length of #16 stem wire. Wrap and glue the tip with thin strips of white tissue paper. Cover only about an inch.

Place a small amount of glue at the base of a small petal on its ironed side. Wrap it around the paper-covered tip of the stem wire to form a cylinder. Place small amounts of glue on the bases of two other small petals and alternately overlap them around the first one, ironed sides inward. Place a small amount of glue on the base of a calyx and wrap it

around the base of the petals. Wrap the stem wire with floral tape down for about 2 inches.

To make a partially opened flower, start with a bud on an 8-inch length of #18 stem wire. Add two more small petals so that there are five small petals in all. Add the calyx. Wrap the stem wire with green floral tape, starting at the calyx and moving down about 2 inches.

To make the large flower,

start with a partially opened flower at the tip of a 4-inch length of #18 stem wire. Then add five large petals, ironed sides inward, alternately overlapping them at the base. Add the calyx and wrap the stem wire with green floral tape.

To assemble the flowers, start by finishing the bud's stem. Wrap its stem with green floral tape, adding a few small leaves and then a few large ones while wrapping. Next take the stem wire for the partially opened flower and attach it to the bud's stem with the floral tape. Add small and large leaves while wrapping. About halfway down the stem, add the large flower. Continue wrapping the stem wires together with the tape to the end.

CHAPTER 12

CATTLEYA

*T*he cattleya (of the family Orchidaceae, the largest flower family, with over 20,000 known species) is one of the largest and most colorful of the orchids. The lip of this sensual flower is very unusual and beautiful. The colors of the petals range from white to yellow, pink, and lavender, with brilliant pink, yellow, and purple lips.

Materials

silk: white
velvet: white
cotton (optional)
dyes: pink or lavender (optional),
    green, yellow, yellowish
    green, purple (optional)
markers: purple, pink, lavender,
    or rose (optional)
pink or purple cloth-covered wire:
    #30
green cloth-covered wire: #30
stem wire: #16
thin strips of tissue paper
floral tape: green

Assembly

1 flower
1 leaf

If using silk, all the petals and the leaf are to be of double thickness, so you will be doubling your

12-1. Cattleya.

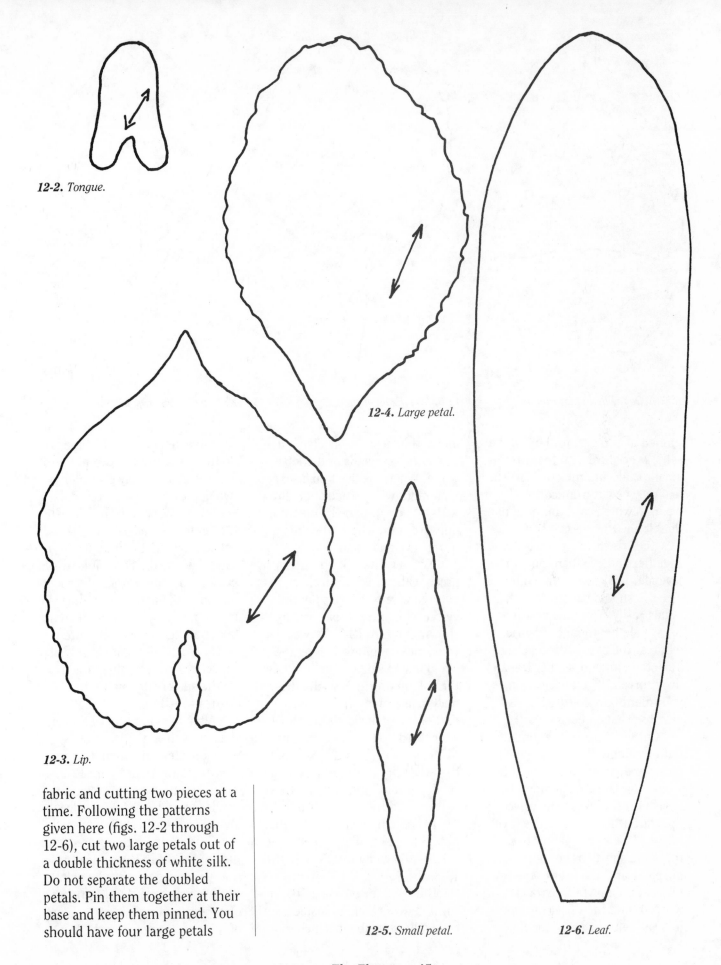

12-2. *Tongue.*

12-4. *Large petal.*

12-3. *Lip.*

12-5. *Small petal.*

12-6. *Leaf.*

fabric and cutting two pieces at a time. Following the patterns given here (figs. 12-2 through 12-6), cut two large petals out of a double thickness of white silk. Do not separate the doubled petals. Pin them together at their base and keep them pinned. You should have four large petals

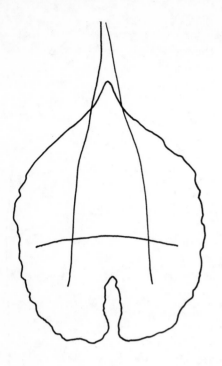

12-7. *Wire the lip trellis fashion.*

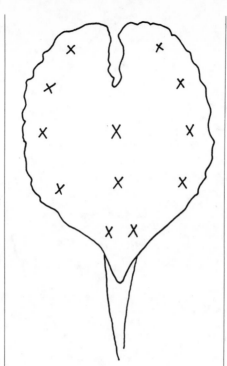

12-8. *Iron the lip at the Xs.*

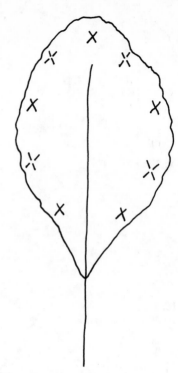

12-9. *Iron each large petal at the Xs.*

pinned in two groups. Follow the same procedure with the three small petals and the one leaf. The leaf may be cut from cotton if you wish, in which case you need not double the thickness.

Keep the petals pinned together and dye them pink or lavender (or leave them white). The dye should penetrate both petals easily. You might wish to leave a slight amount of fabric white at the base of each petal. Take the pinned-together leaf and dye it green. If you use cotton, you might have to turn the leaf over to dye its other side.

Cut one lip and one tongue out of a single thickness of white velvet and cut another lip out of white silk. Dye the tongue yellowish green. To dye the velvet lip, start at its apex and dye it yellowish green, then yellow below that. Add short strokes of pink or purple near the center of the two lobes of the lip. Take extra care when dyeing the velvet lip, since it is the centerpiece of the flower

and is the most visible element. Leave the very ends of the lobes white. When the dyed lip dries, you might wish to add short lines with a colored marker branching outward from where the pink or purple dye ends.

Now dye the silk lip yellowish green. Glue pink or purple cloth-covered wire to the back of the velvet lip in a trellis pattern, as shown in figure 12-7. Now apply a thin smear of glue all along the wired (back) side of the lip. Place the silk lip over this so that they match, and press firmly. Since part of the back side is visible after the flower is finished, this hides the wiring on the back of the velvet lip. With scissors, make small slits along the two lip lobes to give a ruffled and fringed look.

Iron the lip by pressing with a heated knife handle on the velvet side, as shown by the *X*s in figure 12-8.

Glue pink or purple cloth-covered wire carefully inside each petal, allowing about 2 inches of

wire to extend below the base. To do this, separate the two pieces of each petal and apply glue along two opposite sides of cloth-covered wire. Place the wire along the center of one piece of the petal, allowing 2 inches of wire to extend below the base. Take the petal's mate and carefully place it on top of the first so that they match perfectly. Press with your finger along the wire. Be sure the petals are glued together only at the wire. Applying glue directly on the silk creates stains and destroys the look.

After the glue is dry between the petals, iron the large ones with a heated knife handle, as shown by the *X*s in figure 12-9. Then iron the large and small petals with a heated knife edge, as shown in figure 12-10.

Glue green cloth-covered wire inside the leaf in the same way that you glued wire to the petals. Be sure you have about 2 inches of wire extending below the base of the leaf. Do not iron the leaf.

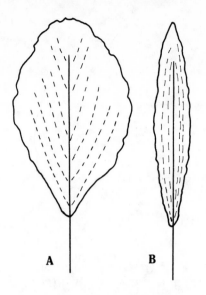

12-10. *Iron the veins of the small and large petals on the dashed lines.*

Next glue green cloth-covered wire to the back side of the tongue. Then apply a small amount of glue on the back side

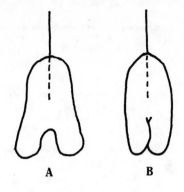

12-11. (A) *Tongue.* (B) *Overlap tongue lobes so that they create a bulge.*

of one tongue lobe and overlap the lobes slightly to form a small bulge. (See fig. 12-11.)

To assemble the finished flower, start with the tongue. Connect it to the tip of a length of #16 stem wire by wrapping and gluing the wires with thin strips of tissue paper. Bend the

tongue downward slightly. Below the tongue add the lip, velvet side up. Add the one large petal on each side of the tongue. Secure all these to the stem wire with glue and thin strips of tissue paper. Below the large petals add one small petal extending upward at a forty-five-degree angle and two small petals extending downward at a forty-five-degree angle. Secure these with thin strips of tissue paper and glue. Wrap the base of the flower with green floral tape down about 6 inches.

Bend the stem wire slightly below the flower so that the wire bulges out and makes the flower more visible. Finish the flower by wrapping a few more inches down the stem wire with floral tape. Add the leaf and continue wrapping with the tape to the end of the stem wire.

CHAPTER 13

PHALAENOPSIS ORCHID

The phalaenopsis, sometimes called the moth orchid, is an unusual and spectacular flower. (There are around forty known species in the genus *Phalaenopsis.*) The flower spikes generally are short and can have one or many long-lived blossoms, with thick leaves at the base. These small orchids are especially beautiful when used as wedding flowers.

13-1. Phalaenopsis orchid.

Materials
silk: white
velvet
cotton (optional)
dyes: pink, yellowish green, green, burgundy (optional)
cloth-covered wire to match the lip: #30
cloth-covered wire to match the petals: #30
green cloth-covered wire: #30
absorbent cotton
thin strips of tissue paper
stem wire: #18
floral tape: green

Assembly
3 flowers
3 leaves

Following the patterns given here (figs. 13-2 through 13-7), cut three lips and six large petals out of silk. Cut nine small petals out of silk. Cut three leaves, three tongues, and three lip petals out of cotton, velvet, or silk. Cut three more lips out of velvet.

Dye the silk petals very pale pink or leave them white. Dye the

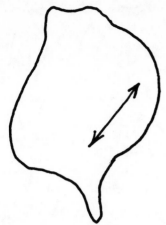

13-2. *Large petal.*

13-3. *Small petal.*

13-5. *Tongue.*

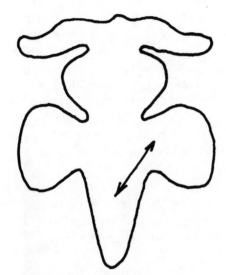

13-4. *Lip.*

13-6. *Lip petal.*

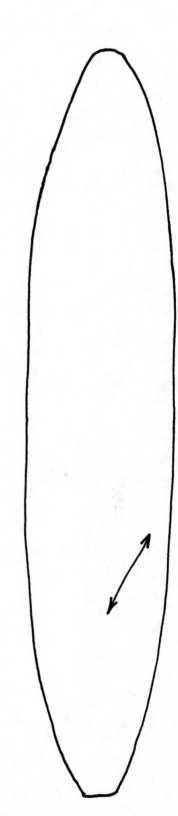

13-7. *Leaf.*

center of the velvet lips pale yellowish green and the edges pink or burgundy. Carefully dye the tongue and lip petals pale yellowish green, or dye them the same color as the petals. Dye the leaves green and the silk lips pale yellowish green.

Very carefully glue green cloth-covered wire on the back side of the velvet lip, as shown in figure 13-8. Be sure to let about 2 inches of wire extend below the pointed end. Apply a thin smear of glue all along the wire back of the velvet lip. Place the silk lip over this so the lips match and press them together firmly along the wire. This will hide the wired side of the velvet lip, since part of it is visible when the flower is finished.

Glue cloth-covered wire along the center of each silk petal, allowing about 2 inches of wire to extend below the base. Glue green cloth-covered wire along the center of each leaf, allowing about 2 inches of wire to extend below the base. Glue green cloth-covered wire on each small lip petal, letting 2 inches of wire extend below one end.

Take a 5-inch length of green

13-8. *Wire the velvet lip in a crosswise fashion.*

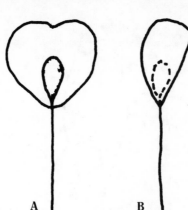

13-9. (A) *Unfolded tongue.* (B) *Tongue folded around absorbent cotton.*

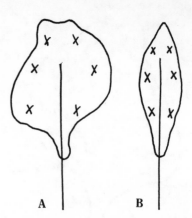

13-10. *Iron the petals at the Xs.* (A) *Large petal.* (B) *Small petal.*

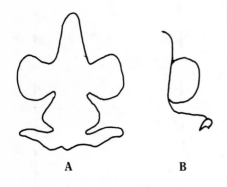

13-11. (A) *Front view of lip before bending.* (B) *Profile of shape of lip.*

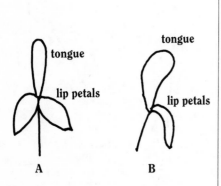

13-12. *Assemble two small lip petals and the tongue.* (A) *Front.* (B) *Profile.*

cloth-covered wire and wrap absorbent cotton around its tip to make a small ball. Apply a thin coat of glue on the surface of the tongue (back or velvet side) (fig. 13-9A) and fold it around the absorbent cotton (fig. 13-9B).

Iron the large and small petals with a heated knife handle on the wired side, as shown by the *X*s in figure 13-10. Do not iron the lip—shape it by bending the wires. With the wired side down, bend the side "wings" up and bend the point at one end downward. Now bend the "horns" of the lip upward. (See fig. 13-11.)

To assemble one flower, take two small lip petals and place one on each side of the tongue, as shown in fig. 13-12. Secure with tissue paper. Then take the lip and put it below the tongue with the unwired side up. Place the large petals beside the tongue, unwired sides out, and a small petal extending upward between the two large petals. Secure with tissue paper. Then place two

small petals below the large petals so they extend downward at forty-five-degree angles.

Wrap the base of the flower with thin strips of tissue paper and secure it to an 18-inch length of #18 stem wire. Starting below the flower, wrap down the stem about 4 inches with green floral tape. Make two more flowers, following the same instructions, and secure them with green floral tape to 5-inch lengths of #18 stem wire.

To assemble the three flowers on a spike, continue wrapping down the stem of the first flower with the floral tape. Add the other two flowers as you wrap. Attach the three leaves about 8 inches from the bottom of the stem wire. All of the leaves are secured to the stem wire at the same place to make what is called a rosette of leaves. Since these orchids lean to the side, you might wish to bend the spike sideways. Or the spike of flowers can droop downward in a flower arrangement.

CHAPTER 14

CYMBIDIUM ORCHID

*T*he genus *Cymbidium* has about seventy species and over a thousand cultivated hybrids. The species of *Cymbidium* made here is a large, bold flower that is very striking yet very delicate. Figure 14-1 does not show the leaves of the Cymbidium orchid, but the pattern shows their size and shape.

Materials

silk: white
cotton (optional)
velvet
dyes: pink, burgundy, yellowish green, green
pink cloth-covered wire: #30
green cloth-covered wire: #30
absorbent cotton
stem wire: #16
thin strips of tissue paper
floral tape: green

Assembly

1 flower
3 leaves

Following the patterns given here (figs. 14-2 through 14-6), cut five petals out of a double thickness of silk. Keep the petal sets paired and pinned at the base (only the petals are doubled). Cut three leaves out of silk or cotton.

14-1. *Cymbidium orchid.*

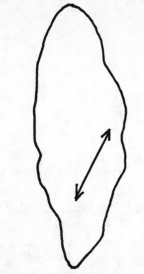

14-2. *Petal.*

14-3. *Lip petal.*

14-5. *Tongue.*

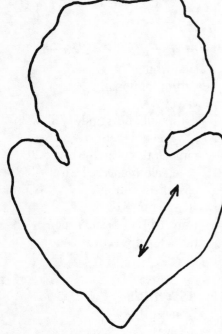

14-4. *Lip.*

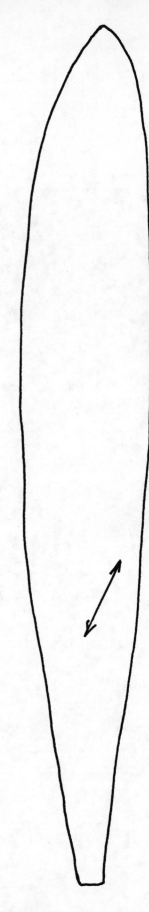

Cut one each of the lip and tongue out of velvet and one other lip out of silk. Cut two lip petals out of velvet.

Dye each petal pale pink, making the color deeper at the base. The dye will penetrate both thicknesses of the petals, so keep them pinned. To make longitudinal streaks on the petals, dip a very fine brush in the pink dye and run it carefully along the petal, creating four or five thin streaks.

Dye the base of the velvet lip deep burgundy, gradually lightening the color to pink as you approach the outer edge. Make small specks of pink or burgundy near the outer edge and blend them in carefully with a piece of cotton. Dye the silk lip and the tongue yellowish green and the leaves green. Dye the lip petals burgundy and make small, dark speckles with quick dabs of a fine brush.

Glue green cloth-covered wire to the back of the velvet lip (fig. 14-7). Then apply a thin smear of glue all over the wired side of the

14-6. *Leaf.*

14-7. *Use an extra V-shaped wire to support the lip.*

14-8. *Sandwich absorbent cotton between two lip petals.*

14-9. *Iron the lip at the Xs.*

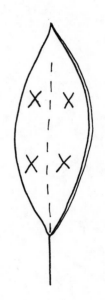

14-10. *Iron the petals at the Xs.*

lip. Take the silk lip and place it over the back side of the velvet lip so that it matches. Press firmly. This will hide the wired side of the velvet lip, since part of the back side is visible after the flower is finished.

Glue two lengths of green cloth-covered wire along the center of each leaf, allowing 2 inches of wire to extend below the base. (Glue these wires right next to each other to give more support to the long leaves and to eliminate limpness.) Carefully glue pink cloth-covered wire inside the petal sets, allowing 2 inches of wire to extend below the base. Apply glue to two opposite sides of the wire and attach the wire to one petal, then place its mate on top symmetrically. Press your finger along the wire to be sure the petals are glued together thoroughly. Do not apply glue to any other part of the petals. Glue green cloth-covered wire on the back of each lobe of the tongue,

allowing 2 inches of wire to extend below the base. Take a 6-inch length of doubled cloth-covered wire and wrap its tip with absorbent cotton. Apply glue along the entire back side of one lip petal and put the absorbent cotton over this. Apply glue along the entire back side of the other lip petal and place it over the first petal. Make sure the absorbent cotton is between the lip petals, and press them together. (See fig. 14-8.)

Iron the lip and petals with a heated knife handle, as shown by the *X*s in figures 14-9 and 14-10. Start ironing the lip at its base on the unwired side.

To assemble the flower, place the tongue on top of the lip and secure their wires to the end of a length of #16 stem wire with thin strips of tissue paper and glue. Curve the lobes of the tongue downward. Next attach the lip petals on top of the tongue and bend the lip petals downward. Attach the flower petals, one extending upward and the four others at forty-five-degree angles at the sides. Secure all the petals to the stem wire with thin strips of tissue paper and glue. Wrap over the tissue and down the stem with green floral tape. Attach the three leaves together

to form a rosette as you wrap with floral tape.

The cymbidium grows with several flowers to a stem and a cluster of leaves near the base of the stem. The stem leans out to the side or droops downward. To achieve this realistic look, make a few more flowers and add them to alternate sides of your stem as you wrap with floral tape. Cymbidiums without leaves can be added to wedding flowers or other arrangements to give them an elegance without flashiness.

CHAPTER 15

MINIATURE ORCHID

15-1. *Miniature orchid.*

*M*iniature orchids are members of a wide variety of orchid species. Many different kinds of these smaller orchids exist, in a wide variety of colors. The miniature orchid created here is a compilation based on several existing species.

Materials
silk: white, green (optional)
velvet
dyes: pink, yellowish green,
    yellow, green (optional)
marker: rose
stem wire: #20, #18
floral tape: yellow, green

Assembly
6 flowers
8 leaves

Following the patterns given here (figs. 15-2 through 15-4), cut six petal sets out of white silk. Cut six throats out of velvet. Cut eight leaves out of white or green silk.

Dye the center of each petal set yellowish green and the lobes pink. Dye the narrow base of each throat yellow, the rest of it pink. To deepen the color of the throat's wavy edge, use a rose marker to make streaks radiating

54

15-2. *Petal.*

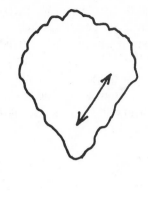

15-3. *Throat.*

15-4. *Leaf.*

15-5. *Rose-colored streaks radiate outward on the throat.*

15-6. *Iron each petal set at the Xs.*

15-7. *Iron each leaf at the Xs.*

outward from its center after it is dry (fig. 15-5). Dye the leaves green (if you cut them from white silk).

Iron the petal sets, leaves, and throats with a heated knife handle, as shown by the *X*s in figures 15-6, 15-7, and 15-8.

To make one flower take a 3-inch length of #20 stem wire. Wrap yellow floral tape about ½ inch down from the tip. Apply glue to the front side of a throat at the narrow base. Wrap this section of the throat around the tip of the stem wire near the yellow floral tape, forming a cone. Glue

the overlapping edges. Bend the wavy edge of the throat downward. (See fig. 15-9.)

Pierce a petal set in the center on the ironed side with an awl. This hole should be big enough so you can slip the petal set partway up the throat. Apply a small amount of glue around the hole on the ironed side and slip the wire through the hole. Slide the petals up so they are secured partway up the throat. Wrap below the petals and down the short stem with green floral tape. Make five more of these flowers. Make one of these five flowers at

15-8. *Iron each throat at the Xs.*

the tip of a 12-inch length of #18 stem wire, which will become the main stem.

To assemble the flowers, wrap

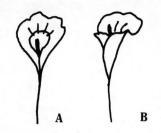

15-9. *Throat.* (A) *Front view.* (B) *Profile.*

green floral tape below the flower at the tip of the main stem. Add a leaf or two as you wrap. These leaves are easy to attach to the stem if you pinch and twist them at their bases to form tiny stems, which then can be wrapped to the main stem wire. Add the other flowers and leaves alternately as you wrap down the stem with green floral tape. When adding flowers, try to attach them to the stem so that the throat is visible at the lower part of the flower. This allows you to look down into the deep fold of the throat. Place the leaves on the stem so that most of them droop downward.

CHAPTER 16

CAMELLIA

*T*he camellia (of the family Theaceae) is one of the few flowers whose beauty can compete with that of the rose. It has only the barest fragrance—in fact, for centuries it was thought to be odorless. In flower language the camellia means unsimulated excellence.

Materials
silk: white
starch
3-inch-wide satin ribbon: green
dye: pink
green cloth-covered wire: #30
commercial stamen: yellow
thin strips of tissue paper
stem wire: #16, #18, #20
absorbent cotton
floral tape: green

Assembly
1 flower
2 buds
6 leaves
6 calyxes

Following the patterns given here (figs. 16-2 through 16-5), cut five small petals and eight large ones out of starched white silk. Cut six leaves and six calyxes out of wide green satin ribbon. Cut two bud triangles out of white silk.

16-1. *Camellia.*

57

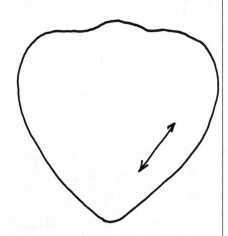

16-2. *Large petal.*

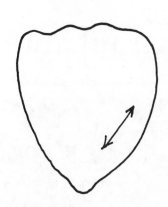

16-3. *Small petal.*

16-4. *Calyx.*

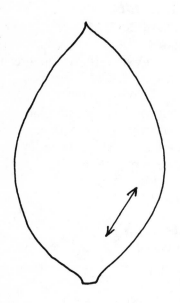

16-5. *Leaf.*

16-6. *Iron the large petal at the Xs.*

16-7. *Iron the calyx at the Xs.*

Dye the petals pale pink. Make the color deeper at the bases of the petals. Dye the bud triangles pale pink. If you prefer, the petals and buds may be left white.

Glue green cloth-covered wire along the center of each leaf, allowing 2 inches of wire to extend below the base.

Iron the wired side of each leaf with a heated knife edge, showing a simple branching vein structure. Iron the petals and calyxes with a heated knife handle, as shown by the *X*s in figures 16-6 and 16-7.

Make a stamen cluster by taking about twenty yellow commercial stamen and wrapping

#30 stem wire around the middle of their stems. Bend the ends of the stamens upward and wrap the base of the cluster with thin strips of tissue paper and glue (fig. 16-8). Attach the stamen to the tip of a 12- to 18-inch length of #16 stem wire by wrapping with thin strips of tissue paper and glue (fig. 16-9).

To make the flower, apply glue to the ironed side at the base of each of the small petals. Place the petals around the base of the stamen cluster so they overlap. Next apply glue to the unironed side at the base of each of the large petals. Place these around the small petals so they overlap.

Pierce the center of a calyx with an awl on the ironed side and apply glue near this hole on the same side. Slip the flower's stem wire through the hole in the calyx on the ironed side and slide the calyx up to secure it below the flower. Then attach one more calyx below the first one in just the same way, making the sepals overlap. Wrap about ½ inch below the calyx with green floral tape. Then attach three leaves all at the same place right below the

16-8. *Wrap wire around the stamens at their centers.*

16-9. *Wrap tissue paper around the base of the stamens.*

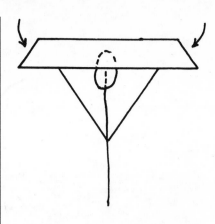

16-10. *Fold the bud triangle over the cotton ball.*

16-11. *Tie off the fabric just below the bulge.*

16-12. *Place two leaves right below the two buds.*

flower. Wrap down the stem a few more inches with the floral tape.

Next make two buds. Wrap absorbent cotton around the tip of a 6-inch length of #18 stem wire. Fold the base (the long edge) of a bud triangle down about 1 inch and slip the cotton under the fold (fig. 16-10). Bring the corners of the triangle down and around and twist at the base of the bud. Wrap the base of the bud with #30 stem wire or strips of tissue paper and glue (fig. 16-11). Trim off any excess fabric below the bud (without cutting the stem wire).

Pierce the center of a calyx with an awl and apply a thin smear of glue over the entire calyx on the ironed side. Slide the calyx up under the bud—be sure

the sepals are glued securely to the bud. This gives the bud a "tight" look. Add one more calyx in just the same way so that its sepals alternate with the sepals of the first calyx.

Make another bud on a very short (about 4-inch) piece of #18 stem wire. Wrap these two buds together with green floral tape and add two leaves right below the buds (fig. 16-12). Wrap down the bud stem a few more inches and add one more leaf.

To finish the flower, continue wrapping below the flower with green floral tape. Add the buds' stem as you wrap to the end of the main stem wire with green floral tape.

CHAPTER 17

POINSETTIA

*T*hese popular plants (of the genus *Euphorbia)* come in two colors, dark red and white. They have a festive look and make excellent decorative plants for the holidays. The beautiful large blossoms of this flower are not actually petals—they are called bracts. The very centers of the blossoms are the flowers, and their fragrance is insignificant because of their relatively small size.

Materials
silk: white, red (optional)
dyes: green, red (optional)
green cloth-covered wire: #30
cloth-covered wire to match the
    bracts: #30
commercial or handmade poin-
    settia peps
stem wire: #16
thin strips of tissue paper
floral tape: green

Assembly
1 blossom
3 small leaves
2 large leaves
5 center flowers (peps)

It is sometimes difficult to start with white silk and dye it a brilliant red. If you prefer red

17-1. *Poinsettia.*

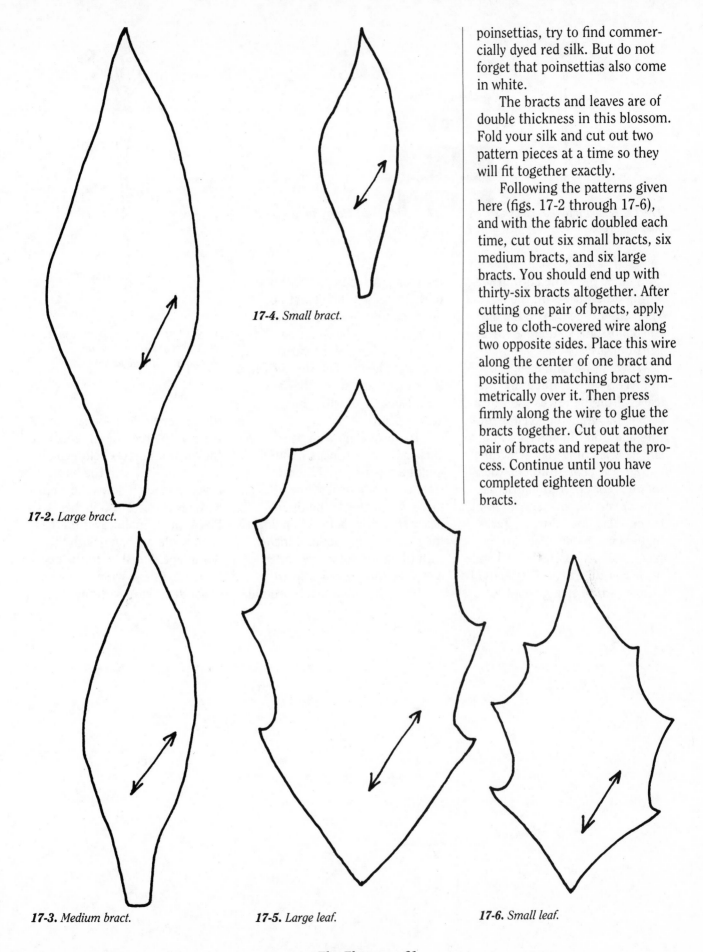

poinsettias, try to find commercially dyed red silk. But do not forget that poinsettias also come in white.

The bracts and leaves are of double thickness in this blossom. Fold your silk and cut out two pattern pieces at a time so they will fit together exactly.

Following the patterns given here (figs. 17-2 through 17-6), and with the fabric doubled each time, cut out six small bracts, six medium bracts, and six large bracts. You should end up with thirty-six bracts altogether. After cutting one pair of bracts, apply glue to cloth-covered wire along two opposite sides. Place this wire along the center of one bract and position the matching bract symmetrically over it. Then press firmly along the wire to glue the bracts together. Cut out another pair of bracts and repeat the process. Continue until you have completed eighteen double bracts.

17-4. *Small bract.*

17-2. *Large bract.*

17-3. *Medium bract.*

17-5. *Large leaf.*

17-6. *Small leaf.*

17-7. *Attach yarn to the end of a 3-inch piece of wire.*

17-8. *Add baker's clay to form a hand-made pep.*

17-9. *Cluster the peps, add a few commercial stamens, and wrap the base with thin strips of tissue paper.*

Follow the same cutting and wiring procedure with the leaves. There are five leaves on the finished blossom, so there are five pairs of leaves to cut.

Use a heated knife edge to iron veins on the bracts and the leaves. Iron the leaves showing a compound branching vein structure and iron the bract showing a simple branching vein structure.

For the center flowers, you may use commercial poinsettia peps or you can make them from baker's clay (see "Further Techniques" in Chapter 2 for the recipe for baker's clay). For handmade peps, use six fine strands of yellow yarn or string about ½ inch long. Attach them with glue to the tip of a 3-inch length of green cloth-covered wire (fig. 17-7). Mold the baker's clay around the base of the yarn strands to form a ball (fig. 17-8). Bake them, and when they are cool, paint them with green acrylic paint.

To make a blossom, first cluster the center peps. (You might also wish to add some smaller commercial stamen.) Place the cluster at the tip of heavy stem wire #16. Wrap down the stem for only about 2 inches with thin strips of tissue paper and glue. (See fig. 17-9.)

Place the small bracts around the center flowers and secure them with green floral tape. Place the medium bracts below these and wrap. End with the large bracts and wrap down the stem wire for about 2 or 3 inches. Place three small leaves on the stem while wrapping with the floral tape. Finish with the two large leaves and wrap to the end of the stem wire with the tape.

CHAPTER 18

RHODODENDRON

*T*he rhododendron (of the family Ericaceae) grows in both tree and shrub forms and has long been the flower of choice among British gardeners because its many blossoms and foliage do well in colder weather. There are a great many rhododendron hybrids, and their number is increased constantly by industrious horticulturists. Norse mythology carries many references to the rhododendron as the flower of the giants.

Materials
silk: white
cotton (optional)
starch
dyes: yellowish green, green, pink (optional)
green cloth-covered wire: #30
commercial stamen: white
stem wire: #16, #18
thin strips of tissue paper
floral tape: green

Assembly
7 flowers
2 partially opened flowers
9 calyxes
10 leaves

Following the patterns given here (figs. 18-2 through 18-4), cut nine sets of petals out of

18-1. Rhododendron.

18-3. Calyx.

18-2. Petal set.

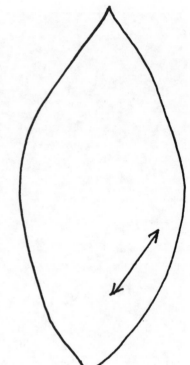

18-4. Leaf.

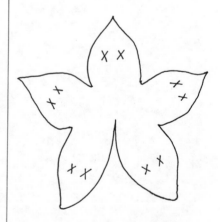

18-5. Iron each petal set at the Xs.

starched white silk. Cut 10 leaves and nine calyxes out of starched silk or cotton.

Dye the center of each petal set yellowish green. Dye the edges of the petal lobes pale pink, or leave them white. Dye the leaves and calyxes green. If you are using pink dye for the petals, dye the sepal tips of each calyx pink to accent them.

Glue green cloth-covered wire along the center of each leaf, allowing 2 inches of wire to extend below the base.

Iron each leaf on the wired side with a heated knife edge, showing a simple branching vein structure. Iron each petal set with a heated knife handle, as shown by the *X*s in figure 18-5.

Make stamen clusters for seven flowers. Cut off the ends on about eight commercial stamen. (If you are making pink flowers, you might wish to dab a little

pink dye on the tips of the stamen if they will absorb dye.) Place the stamen at the tip of a 5-inch piece of #18 stem wire. Secure them to the wire by wrapping with thin strips of tissue paper and glue (fig. 18-6).

To make one flower, take a petal set and hold it ironed side down. Following the sequence shown in figure 18-7, bring petal lobe 1 inside and turn it so it is situated between petal lobes 3 and 4. Glue petal lobe 5 on the outside between petal lobes 2 and 3. This makes the petal lobes appear to be overlapping.

Now pierce the center of the flower with an awl. Apply glue to the base of one of the stamen clusters and insert it in the top of the flower through the hole. The base of the stamen cluster should rest on the base of the flower. Apply glue at the base of a calyx and wrap it around the base of

the flower. Wrap below the flower and down the stem with green floral tape.

To make a partially opened flower, follow the same procedure

18-6. *Wrap the stamen cluster with tissue paper.*

18-7. *Attach petal lobe 1 between lobes 3 and 4.*

as for the flower, but hold the set of petals ironed side up. This way, all petal lobes will curve inward. Instead of slipping a stamen cluster through the center of the flower, just wrap the tip of a 5-inch piece of #18 stem wire with green floral tape and slip this through the center of the flower. Glue on the calyx and wrap below the flower and down the wire with green floral tape.

After you have made seven flowers and two partially opened flowers, you are ready to assemble them on the main stem. Take four flowers and one partially opened flower and place all of them at the tip of an 18-inch piece of #16 stem wire. Secure them to the wire by wrapping with thin strips of tissue paper and glue. Wrap over the tissue and down the stem wire for about 3 inches with green floral tape. Then position five leaves in one place so the leaves extend out in a leaf rosette. Bend the flower stems out at slight angles. Next take an 8-inch piece of #18 stem wire and arrange the remaining flowers at its tip in the same way. Wrap about 3 inches down the stem wire with green floral tape and attach five leaves so that they overlap alternately in a rosette arrangement. Place the #18 stem next to the #16 stem and wrap them together with floral tape. Wrap to the end of the longer stem wire with the tape.

CHAPTER 19

AZALEA

*T*he azalea is in the same family (Ericaceae) as the rhododendron. Most azalea hybrids originated in Japan, although a few started in Europe. They are generally evergreen and grow to a moderate height.

Materials
silk: white
cotton (optional)
dyes: yellowish green, green, orange or pink or yellow
commercial stamen: white or yellow
stem wire: #16, #20
thin strips of tissue paper
floral tape: green

Assembly
6 flowers
6 calyxes
13 leaves

Following the patterns given here (figs. 19-2 through 19-4), cut twelve petal sets out of silk. Cut thirteen leaves and six calyxes out of silk or cotton.

Dye the center of each petal set yellowish green. Dye the petals orange, pink, or yellow, or leave them white. Dye the leaves and calyxes green. Dab a little dye on the stamen tips (the same

19-1. *Azalea.*

19-2. *Petal set.*

19-3. *Leaf.*

19-4. *Calyx.*

19-5. *Iron each petal set at the Xs.*

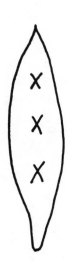

19-6. *Iron each leaf at the Xs.*

19-7. *Wrap the stamen cluster with tissue paper.*

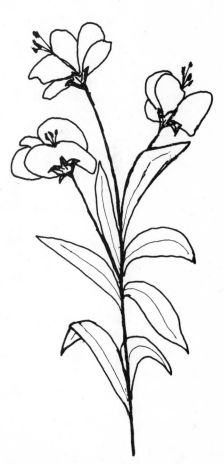

19-8. *Attach the leaves so that most of them droop.*

color that you use for the petals).

Iron each petal set and leaf with a heated knife handle, as shown by the *X*s in figures 19-5 and 19-6.

To prepare a stamen cluster, cut off one end of about six stamen. Attach them to a 5-inch length of #20 stem wire with thin strips of tissue paper and glue (fig. 19-7). Make six of these clusters.

Put a small amount of glue in the center of a petal set on the ironed side. Then place another petal set on top of the first, ironed side up, so that their centers match and their petals are alternating. With an awl, pierce a hole in the center of the doubled petal set on the unironed side. Apply more glue near this hole on the unironed side and insert the stamen cluster through the hole. Slide up the doubled petal set so it rests near the base of the stamen cluster. Pinch the petal set at the base below the stamen to gather the petals up and around the stamen. Apply glue to the base of a calyx and wrap it around the base of the flower. Wrap below the flower and down its stem with green floral tape. Make six of these flowers.

To assemble the flowers on the main stem, take three flowers and place them near each other at the tip of a 12-inch piece of #16 stem wire. Secure them to the stem wire with green floral tape, wrapping only about 2 inches down the stem. Take several leaves and pinch and twist each one at its base to form a tiny "stem." Wrap the leaves on the stem wire one at a time near each other. Place the leaves on the stem so that most of them droop downward, as shown in figure 19-8. Wrap on about six leaves. Wrap about 3 inches below the leaves with the floral tape. Take a 6- to 8-inch length of #20 stem wire, attach three flowers to its tip, and wrap on a cluster of leaves below the flowers. Attach this to the main stem with green floral tape. Add any extra leaves as you wrap to the end of the main stem with the tape.

CHAPTER 20

SWEET PEA

*T*he modern sweet pea (genus *Lathyrus*) comes in a great variety of colors and is much larger than the original sweet pea, which originated in Sicily. Unfortunately, much of the original delicious scent for which it was named has been lost through hybridization. The sweet pea is easy to grow and thrives in a variety of garden settings.

Materials
silk: white
cotton (optional)
starch
dyes: green, yellowish green, wide choice of petal colors
green cloth-covered wire: #30
floral tape: green
stem wire: #18

Assembly
3 flowers
2 buds
6 or 7 leaves
5 calyxes
1 tendril

Following the patterns given here (figs. 20-2 through 20-5), cut six large petals and five small petals out of starched white silk. Cut six or seven leaves and five calyxes out of silk or cotton.

20-1. Sweet pea.

69

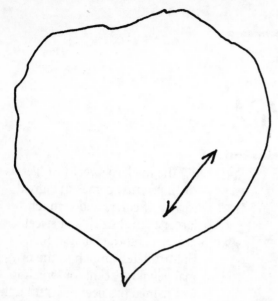

20-2. *Large petal.*

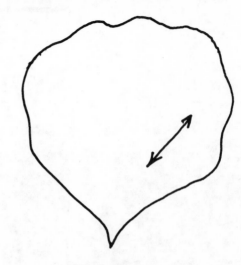

20-3. *Small petal.*

20-4. *Calyx.*

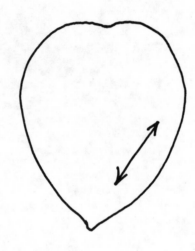

20-5. *Leaf.*

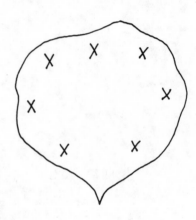

20-6. *Iron each small and large leaf at the Xs.*

Dye the leaves and the calyxes green. Dye the bases of each petal yellowish green and the edges any desired color (such as pink, yellow, pale blue, orange, or lavender).

Glue green cloth-covered wire along the center of each leaf, allowing about 3 inches of wire to extend below the base.

Iron the leaf veins with a heated knife edge, showing a compound branching vein structure on the wired side. Wrap the stem of each leaf with green floral tape.

Iron the large and small petals with a heated knife handle, as shown by the *X*s in figure 20-6. Iron each calyx with a heated knife handle, as shown by the *X*s in figure 20-7.

To make the buds, first wrap about 2 inches of a 6-inch length of #18 stem wire with green floral tape. Make a loop at the wrapped end of the stem wire (fig. 20-8). Apply a small amount of glue at the base of a small petal. Roll the petal around the wire loop (fig. 20-9). Put a small amount of glue at the base of a

20-7. *Iron each calyx at the Xs.*

20-8. *Make a loop in the taped stem wire.*

calyx and wrap the calyx around the base of the small petal (fig. 20-10). Wrap the rest of the stem wire with green floral tape.

To make a flower, make a bud with the small petal but do not add the calyx. Put a small amount of glue on the base of each of two large petals on their unironed (back) sides. Glue these petals together back to back at the base (fig. 20-11). Apply a small amount of glue to the base of one of these glued-together petals and wrap it around the small petal (fig. 20-12). Now apply a small amount of glue to the base of a calyx and wrap it around the base of the flower. Wrap the stem wire with green floral tape.

20-9. *Wrap the petal around the wire loop.*

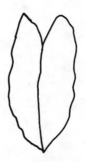

20-11. *Glue large petals back to back.*

Make a tendril by wrapping green cloth-covered wire in a spiral around an awl. When you release it, it retains the spiral shape.

To assemble all of the flowers, start with a bud. Secure it to a

20-10. *Wrap the calyx around the base of the small petal.*

20-12. *On one side of the back-to-back petals, wrap the base of one of the large petals around a small petal.*

12-inch length of #18 stem wire with green floral tape. Attach the tendril, then the other bud, then leaves and flowers all along the length of the stem wire as you wrap to its end with the tape.

CHAPTER 21

MARGUERITE

*T*he marguerite (of the family Compositae) is a type of chrysanthemum that has been cultivated in China since the time of Confucius, around 500 B.C., when it was considered the symbol of life. Introduced into Japan in the third century A.D., it has since become their national flower; a large festival centers on the flower each fall.

Materials
silk: white
velvet
cotton (optional)
dyes: yellow, green
thread
green cloth-covered wire: #30
stem wire: #18
floral tape: green

Assembly
1 flower
1 partially opened flower
2 calyxes
3 leaves
1 stamen strip

Following the patterns given here (figs. 21-2 through 21-5), cut two petal strips out of white silk. With a scissors, make a point at the top of each little petal along each of the strips. Cut three

21-1. Marguerite.

72

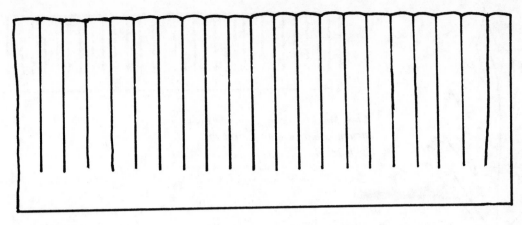

21-2. *Petal strip.*

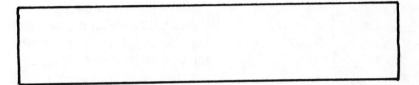

21-3. *Stamen strip.*

21-4. *Calyx.*

21-5. *Leaf.*

leaves, two calyxes, and one stamen strip out of cotton or velvet.

Dye the leaves and calyxes green and the stamen strip yellow. Leave the petal strips white.

Sew running stitches at the base of each petal strip (do not knot or finish off). Then iron each strip with a heated knife handle, as shown by the *X*s in figure 21-6.

Glue green cloth-covered wire in several places on the back side

of each leaf, as shown in figure 21-7. Iron the wired side of each leaf with a heated knife handle, showing a simple branching vein structure.

Make deep snips all along one edge of the stamen strip. Apply glue all along the lower (uncut) edge on the back side. Make a hook at one end of a piece of an 18-inch length of #18 stem wire and hook it onto one end of the stamen strip (fig. 21-8). Roll it up to form a cluster—this becomes the stamen.

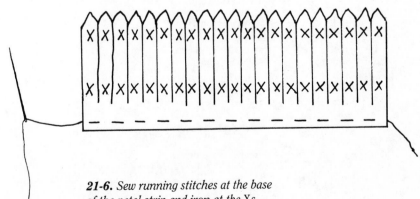

21-6. *Sew running stitches at the base of the petal strip and iron at the Xs.*

21-7. *Wire each leaf in several places.*

21-8. *Make the flower center by hooking stem wire onto a stamen strip and rolling it up.*

To make the flower, apply glue all along the base of a petal strip on the unironed side and pull the thread at the base to gather all the petals tightly. Wrap the petal strip around the base of the stamen without letting the ends of the petal strip overlap. Now pierce the center of a calyx with an awl and smear glue thinly over the back side of the calyx. Slip the stamen's stem wire through the hole on the back side and slide the calyx up and around the base of the flower. Bring up the edges of the calyx to surround the base. Wrap green floral tape below the calyx a few inches down the stem wire.

To make the partially opened flower, apply glue along the base of the ironed side of the other petal strip and pull the thread to gather the petals tightly. Make a small hook at the end of a piece of a 12- to 18-inch length of #18 stem wire and hook the end of the petal strip (as you did with the stamen strip). Wrap the petal strip around the hook. The ends of the strip can overlap. Pierce the center of the other calyx with an awl and apply a thin smear of glue to the back side. Slip the stem wire of the petal strip through the hole and slide the calyx up and around the base of the gathered petal strip. Bring up the edges of the calyx to surround the base. Wrap floral tape a few inches down the stem and add one leaf as you wrap.

To finish the flower, continue wrapping the stem wire of the flower with floral tape. Add the partially opened flower to the stem as you wrap, then the other two leaves. Wrap to the end of the stem wire.

CHAPTER 22

GERANIUM

*T*his flower is commonly called a geranium, although it is in the genus *Pelargonium*. The real geranium, in the genus *Geranium,* is an entirely different flower. Geraniums, whether *Pelargonium* or *Geranium,* are among the world's most popular flowers. In flower language, the geranium signifies gentility.

Materials
silk: red or pink (optional), green (optional), white (optional)
cotton (optional)
starch
dyes: red or pink (optional), green (optional)
marker: red
green cloth-covered wire: #30
stem wire: #16, #18
floral tape: green, plus petal color
20 commercial or handmade geranium peps

Assembly
20 flowers in 2 clusters
3 large leaves
4 small leaves

Following the patterns given here (figs. 22-2 through 22-4), cut twenty petal sets out of starched white, red, or pink silk. Cut three large and four small

22-1. Geranium.

22-2. *Petal set.*

22-3. *Large leaf.*

22-4. *Small leaf.*

leaves out of starched green silk or cotton. If these colors are not available, you can dye the fabric pieces.

Take a red marker and make crescent-shaped streaks on each leaf, as shown in figure 22-5. Use a piece of absorbent cotton to make the color blend in.

Glue green cloth-covered wire on each leaf, allowing 2 inches of wire to extend below the base (fig. 22-6).

Iron each petal set with a heated knife handle, as shown by the *X*s in figure 22-7. Iron each leaf on the wired side with a heated knife edge, showing a compound branching vein structure.

Cut twenty 5-inch lengths of #18 stem wire. Wrap ½ inch at the tip of each with floral tape that is the same color as the petals. This will become the flower center. Pierce the center of a petal set with an awl. Apply glue around the hole on the ironed side and slip the untaped end of the wire through the hole (fig. 22-8). Slide the petals up and pinch them around the floral tape (fig. 22-9). Wrap the base of the flower and down the stem with

green floral tape. Make twenty of these flowers.

Assemble two large flower clusters. Take ten flowers and attach a few of them at a time to the tip of a 12-inch length of #16 stem wire with green floral tape. These flowers should all appear to emerge from the same place at the tip of the stem wire. Now take ten commercial geranium peps, bend them outward slightly, and arrange them around these flowers. (See fig. 22-1.) Attach

22-5. *Make crescent-shaped streaks with a red marker on each leaf.*

22-6. *Add an extra wire to each leaf for support.*

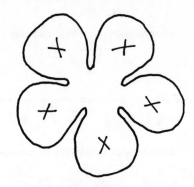

22-7. *Iron each petal set at the Xs.*

22-8. *Insert the stem wire through a hole in the center of the petal set.*

them to the stem with green floral tape. Wrap down the stem a few inches, then add two small leaves.

Make another large flower cluster at the tip of a 10-inch length of #16 stem wire in just the same way.

If commercial geranium peps are not available, you can make your own out of baker's clay. Each pep is about ½ inch long (fig. 22-10). The tips are the same color as the petals and the bulging base is green. (See "Further Techniques" in Chapter 2 for instructions on how to make baker's clay peps and stamen.)

22-9. *The floral tape pinches the petal set around the flower center.*

To complete the project, wrap the two flower-cluster stems together with green floral tape.

22-10. *Handmade geranium pep.*

Add large leaves as you wrap with the tape to the end of the stem wire.

CHAPTER 23

GLADIOLUS

*T*he gladiolus (of the family Iridaceae) is known for its magnificent size and wide variety of colors. With a large number of blossoms arranged on each flower spike, it is an asset to any over-sized bouquet. Pliny the Elder named the flower from the Latin word *gladius,* meaning sword, because of the shape of the leaves.

Materials

silk: white
cotton (optional)
starch
dyes: green, plus wide choice of
    petal colors
stem wire: #18, #12 (or #16)
18 commercial or handmade
    stamen: white and yellow
    (optional)
thin strips of tissue paper
cloth-covered wire to match
    petals: #30
green cloth-covered wire: #30
floral tape: green

Assembly

2 large flowers, 1 medium flower,
    1 partially opened flower, and
    4 buds—all on one stalk
2 large leaves
8 medium leaves
14 small leaves

Following the patterns given here (figs. 23–2 through 23–7),

23-1. *Gladiolus.*

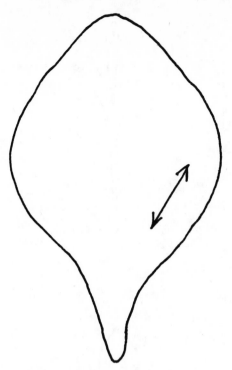

23-2. *Large petal.*

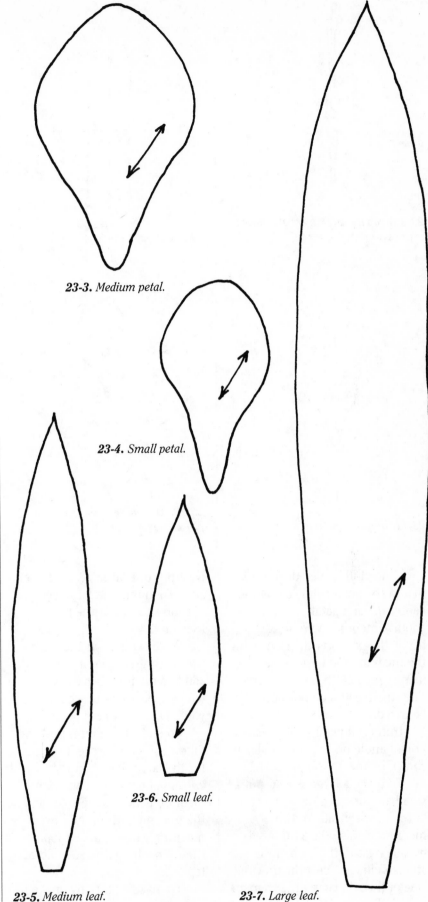

23-3. *Medium petal.*

23-4. *Small petal.*

cut eight large, eight medium, and nine small petals out of starched white silk. Dye them any desired color such as red, yellow, pink, orange, or lavender. Leave each petal's center white near the base—or you can dye the petals a solid color. Cut fourteen small, eight medium, and two large leaves out of silk or cotton. Dye them green.

Make three stamen clusters. Take three round white commercial stamens and cut one end off of each. Attach them to the tip of a 5-inch piece of #18 stem wire by wrapping thin strips of tissue paper and glue around the stamen and stem wire (fig. 23-8). Then take three other commercial stamen in white or yellow and cut them in half (fig. 23-9). Place three of these near the base of the other stamen and secure them all by wrapping with thin strips of tissue paper and glue (fig. 23-10).

23-5. *Medium leaf.*

23-6. *Small leaf.*

23-7. *Large leaf.*

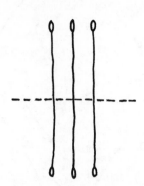

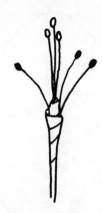

23-8. *Wrap three commercial stamens with tissue paper.*

23-9. *Cut three stamens in half.*

23-10. *Completed stamen cluster wrapped with tissue paper.*

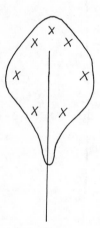

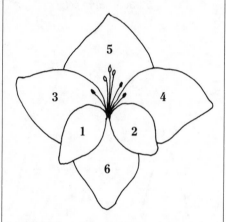

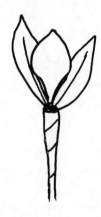

23-11. *Iron each petal at the Xs.*

23-12. *Assemble each flower in the proper sequence.*

23-13. *Finished bud.*

Glue cloth-covered wire (to match the petal color) along the center of each petal, allowing about 2 inches of wire to extend below the base. Do the same with the medium and large leaves, using green cloth-covered wire. The small leaves do not need to be wired.

Iron each petal with a heated knife handle on the wired side, as shown by the *X*s in figure 23-11.

To make a large flower, put a small amount of glue at the base of the unwired side of two medium petals. Place these side by side next to the base of the stamen cluster, with the unwired side of the silk facing the stamen.

Next put one large petal on each side. Then put one large petal at the top and one at the bottom. (See fig. 23-12.) Wrap the base of the flower and down the stem wire with green floral tape, and add two medium leaves as you wrap. Repeat this procedure so you have two large flowers.

To make a medium flower, follow the same procedure used for the large flower, but start with two small petals and add four medium petals at the sides and at the top and bottom. Add two medium leaves while wrapping the stem wire with green floral tape.

To make a partially opened

flower, place three small petals together with wired sides inward. Begin wrapping at the base of the flower with floral tape. Add two small leaves. Since the small leaves have no cloth-covered wire glued to them, they must be secured by wrapping the base of the leaf itself to the petal wire with green floral tape.

To make buds, take one small petal, roll it up loosely, and glue it to two small leaves at the base. Wrap the base of the bud with floral tape (fig. 23-13). Repeat this three times to make four buds.

To assemble the flowers on the gladiolus stalk, you will need

18 inches of heavy (#12) stem wire. (You can substitute three 18-inch lengths of #16 wire bound together by strips of paper or tape.) Start assembling flower stalks at the tip. Add four small leaves alternately while wrapping with green floral tape. When the small leaves are attached, wrap the buds on alternately, then the partially opened flower. You should by now be about one quarter of the way down the stem wire. Next add the medium flower, then the two large flowers, adding any leftover medium leaves along the way. Add the two large leaves. Continue wrapping down the length of the heavy stem wire with green floral tape. To make the flowers look realistic, bend them alternately away from the stem wire.

CHAPTER 24

CHERRY BLOSSOM

*T*he cherry blossom (of the genus *Prunus* of which the peach, the plum, and the almond are also members) is synonymous with a reawakening, with spring. The wild cherry tree has pure white blossoms; the cultivated tree blossoms are tinged with pink.

Materials

silk: white
dyes: pink, brown, green, yellow
    (optional)
commercial stamen: yellow or
    white
stem wire: #16, #18, #26, #30
thin strips of tissue paper
floral tape: green, brown
    (optional)
absorbent cotton

Assembly

4 flowers
5 partially opened flowers
3 buds
12 calyxes

    Following the patterns given here (figs. 24-2 through 24-4), cut nine petals, three bud triangles, and twelve calyxes out of white silk.
    Carefully dye the edges of the petals pale pink. Leave the cen-

24-1. Cherry blossom.

24-2. *Petal.*

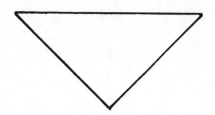

24-3. *Bud triangle.*

24-4. *Calyx.*

ters white. Or you may wish to dye two or three of the petal lobes pink, leaving the other lobes white. Dye the long edge (the base) of each bud triangle pale pink. Dye the center of each calyx green, and accent the tip of each calyx lobe with brown dye. If you cannot find yellow stamen, you can dye some commercial white stamen by dabbing them with a brush dipped in yellow dye.

Iron each petal and each calyx with a heated knife handle, as shown by the *X*s in figures 24-5 and 24-6.

To eliminate bulkiness at the base of each flower, make the stamen clusters carefully. Take about ten stamen and cut them in half. Arrange their "heads" (anthers) so that they have varying heights. Attach them to the tip of a 5-inch piece of #26 stem wire. Secure them to the wire by wrapping with very thin strips of tissue paper and glue (fig. 24-7).

To make a flower, pierce the center of a petal with an awl; the hole should be large enough to encircle the base of a stamen cluster. Apply glue around the hole on the ironed side. Slip the stamen cluster through the hole in the center of the petal and pull the petal up around the stamen. Now pierce the center of a calyx, apply glue around the hole on the ironed side, and slip the flower's stem through the hole in the calyx. Pull the calyx up the stem and secure it below the flower. Cut a piece of green or brown floral tape in half lengthwise (thin strips of floral tape are necessary to eliminate bulkiness) and wrap a strip below the flower and down its stem. Make three more of these flowers.

Partially opened flowers are even easier to make and look just as lovely. Cut a 5-inch length of #26 stem wire and wrap ½ inch of its tip with green floral tape. Pierce the center of a petal with an awl and apply glue around the hole on the ironed side. Slip the stem wire through the hole and

pull the flower up and around the floral tape at the tip of the wire. Pinch the base of the flower to bunch the petals. Add the calyx, following the same procedure used for the flower, and wrap below the flower and down its stem with thin strips of green or brown floral tape. Make four more of these partially opened flowers.

To make the bud, cut a 5-inch length of #26 stem wire and wrap its tip with absorbent cotton so that it is the size of a cotton swab. Fold the long edge of the bud triangle down ½ inch. Slip the cotton-wrapped wire below the fold. (See fig. 24-8.) Bring the corners of the bud triangle forward and wrap and twist at the base of the bud. Wrap and twist #30 stem wire at the base of the bud to secure it. Next, cut off excess fabric beneath the #30

24-5. *Iron each petal at the Xs.*

24-6. *Iron each calyx at the Xs.*

24-7. *Wrap each stamen cluster with tissue paper.*

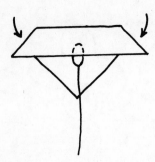

24-8. *Fold the long edge of each bud tri-angle over the cotton-tipped stem wire.*

24-9. *Bud with its calyx.*

wire to eliminate bulkiness below the bud. Wrap the base of the bud with thin strips of tissue paper and glue to secure it to the stem wire. Now pierce the center of a calyx with an awl to form a hole large enough to encircle the base

of the bud. Apply glue thinly on the entire ironed side of the calyx. Slip the bud stem through the hole and pull the calyx up to sur-round the base of the bud so that only the tip of the bud is exposed. Wrap below the bud with thin

strips of green or brown floral tape. (See fig. 24-9.)

Now you are ready to assemble the finished flower. Take a 12-inch length of #16 stem wire and attach the flowers and buds to the tip of the wire in groups of two to four, wrapping with green or brown floral tape. Take two 6-inch lengths of #18 stem wire and do the same, wrap-ping on two to four flowers and buds at a time. Attach these two lengths of #18 stem wire along the main stem as you wrap to the end of the stem wire with green or brown floral tape. Make the flowers look realistic by bending them out at slight angles from the stem.

*Rolled-edged silk iris with
wrinkled petals*

*Fuschia phalaenopsis orchid
and cherry blossoms*

*A variety of the most colorful;
including oriental poppy,
cymbidium orchid, digitalis,
iris and sweetpea*

*Dogwood, anemone, marguerites
and small climbing roses*

*Center of gladiolus stalk
showing rolled-edged petals*

*Bridal bouquet with small
lilies, chrysanthemum and
miniature orchids*

*Corsage with small roses and
miniature orchids*

Boutonniere with buttercup

CHAPTER 25

BOUGAINVILLEA

*T*he bougainvillea (of the genus *Bougainvillaea*) was named after the French explorer Louis de Bougainville. This climbing shrub, a native of South America, comes in a variety of colors ranging from magenta and scarlet to orange, yellow, and white. It is often planted against trellises and arbors, where its dark green leaves and bright blossoms enhance its surroundings.

Materials

silk: white
cotton (optional)
dyes: magenta, green
green cloth-covered wire: #30
magenta cloth-covered wire: #30
small commercial dried flowers:
   white
stem wire: #16, #18 (optional)
floral tape: green
thin strips of tissue paper
commercial peps or stamen:
   brown or magenta
marker: brown or magenta
   (optional)

Assembly

3 blossoms
4 large leaves
4 small leaves

The beautiful and colorful blossoms of the bougainvillea are

25-1. Bougainvillea.

85

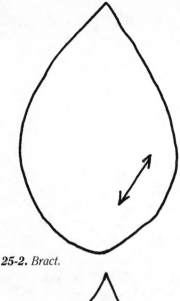

25-2. *Bract.*

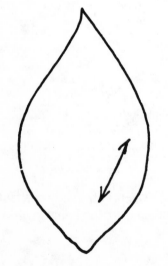

25-3. *Large leaf.*

25-4. *Small leaf.*

botanically referred to as bracts. The plant's actual flowers are the small white flowers in the centers.

If you can obtain a deep magenta color with your dyes, then use white silk; if not, try to buy your silk in this rich color.

Following the patterns given here (figs. 25-2 through 25-4), cut nine bracts out of silk and dye them magenta and cut four small leaves and four large ones out of silk or cotton and dye them green. (You may wish to cut even more leaves to give this climbing plant a very lush look.)

Glue green cloth-covered wire along the center of each leaf, allowing about 2 inches of wire to extend below the base. Glue magenta cloth-covered wire along the center of each bract in a similar fashion.

The vein structure for both bracts and leaves is a simple branching structure. Use a heated knife edge to iron the veins on the wired sides of both bracts and leaves.

To begin the assembly of the bougainvillea blossom, first take two small, dried white flowers. Try to find some with sturdy stems that are at least 4 inches long. Attach them to the tip of a 12-inch piece of #16 stem wire with green floral tape or thin strips of white tissue paper and glue.

Next take two commercial peps or stamen, either brown or magenta. If you cannot find either of these colors, it is easy to color some commercial stamen with a felt marker. Cut off one end of the stamen. Attach them at the sides of the dried flowers and secure them with floral tape or thin strips of tissue and glue. (See fig. 25-5.)

Now arrange the three bracts,

25-5. *Wrap each stamen and flower cluster with thin strips of tissue paper or floral tape.*

wired sides inward, around this central flower cluster. Wrap and secure them to the stem wire right below the central flowers with thin strips of tissue paper and glue. Wrap over this with green floral tape. Curve the bracts inward by bending their wires gently to give the blossom a full, rounded look. Make two more of these blossoms in just the same way on shorter (about 5-inch) lengths of #16 or #18 stem wire. Wrap their stems with green floral tape. Attach a few small leaves to these if you wish.

To assemble the completed blossoms on one stem, start with your first flower on its 12-inch stem wire and finish wrapping down the stem with green floral tape. Add some small leaves, then the other two flowers. Add large leaves while continuing to wrap down the stem with the floral tape.

CHAPTER 26

DIGITALIS

*D*igitalis has been known since ancient times; it was named for its resemblance to a human finger (*digit*). Its common name is foxglove. The plant has long been a staple of folk medicine for chest complaints, but only in modern times has its extract digitalin been used to regulate the heartbeat. There are about twenty-five species in the genus *Digitalis.* In flower language, digitalis signifies insincerity or a wish.

Materials
silk: white (or green and purple or pink)
cotton (optional)
starch
dyes: green and purple or pink (all optional)
purple or pink cloth-covered wire: #30
green cloth-covered wire: #30
thread
acrylic paint: white or cream
marker: brown
48 commercial stamen: white
thin strips of tissue paper
stem wire: #16, #18, #30
floral tape: green
absorbent cotton

Assembly
8 large flowers
8 small flowers
10 buds
26 calyxes
6 leaves

26-1. *Digitalis.*

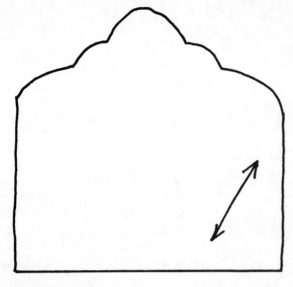

26-2. *Large petal.*

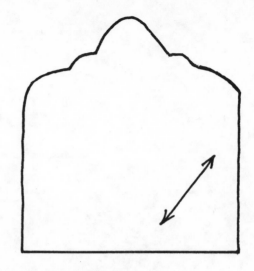

26-3. *Small petal.*

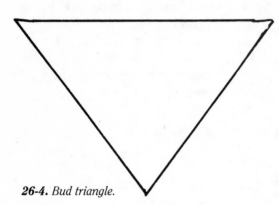

26-4. *Bud triangle.*

26-5. *Calyx.*

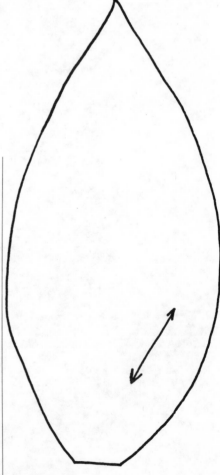

26-6. *Leaf.*

This spectacular flower is very time-consuming to make, but it is well worth the effort. One time-saver is to buy green silk for the leaves and calyxes and purple or pink silk for the flowers and buds instead of using white, to eliminate the dyeing step.

Following the patterns given here (figs. 26-2 through 26-6), cut eight large petals and eight small petals out of starched silk. Also cut ten bud triangles out of silk. Cut six leaves out of starched silk or cotton, with the fabric doubled. Keep the matching leaf pairs pinned at their bases. Cut twenty-six calyxes out of silk or cotton.

Glue purple or pink cloth-covered wire along the edge of each petal, as shown in figure 26-7. To wire the leaves, take green cloth-covered wire and apply glue along two opposite sides of the wire. Place the wire along the center of one leaf of a pair, allowing 2 inches of wire to extend below the base. Take the leaf's mate and place it on top so that it matches. Press along the wire with your finger. The leaf pairs should be glued together at the wire only.

Iron the leaves with a heated knife edge in a simple branching vein structure. Iron the tip of each petal with a heated knife handle, as shown by the *X* in figure 26-8.

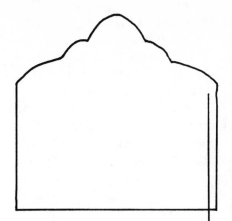

26-7. *Glue wire to the edge of a petal.*

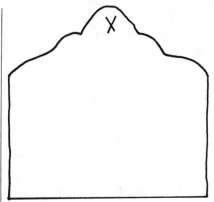

26-8. *Iron each petal at the X.*

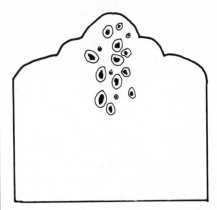

26-9. *Cluster painted markings at the tip of each petal.*

Sew running stitches along the base of each petal. Do not knot or finish off.

Dip a brush in white or cream acrylic paint and make flecks on the unironed side of each petal near the tip. When this dries, color part of the inside of each fleck with a brown marker. (See fig. 26-9.)

Make stamen clusters with 3-inch lengths of #18 stem wire. Take three stamen, fold them in half, and apply glue at the bend. Place the bent part of the stamen at the tip of the stem wire. Secure the stamen to the wire by wrapping with thin strips of tissue paper and glue. Wrap over this

with green floral tape (fig. 26-10). You will need sixteen of these stamen clusters.

To make one flower (large or small), apply glue along the unwired edge of a petal. Then form the petal into a cylinder, allowing about ⅛ inch of the petal's edges to overlap (the petal's wire must be on the inside). Apply a small amount of glue inside the cylinder at the base. Insert stamen through the base of the cylinder. Pull the thread at the base to gather it around the base of the stamen. Apply a small amount of glue to the base of a calyx and wrap the calyx around the base of the flower. Wrap the stem wire below the flower with green floral tape. Now take the purple or pink cloth-covered wire inside the flower and bend it slightly upward, as shown in figure 26-11.

To make a bud, take a 3-inch length of #18 stem wire and wrap the tip with absorbent cotton to

form a small cocoon shape. Fold the long edge (the base) of the bud triangle down ¾ inch and slip the cotton under the fold (fig. 26-12). Bring the corners over and down and wrap and twist the base of the bud. Secure the base of the bud by wrapping it with #30 stem wire. Cut off any excess fabric below the bud to eliminate bulkiness. Apply glue around the base of the bud and wrap the calyx around it. Wrap the stem wire below the bud with green floral tape.

When all flowers, buds, and leaves are finished, you are ready to assemble the digitalis stalk. Take a 20-inch length of #16 stem wire. The digitalis stalk is thick and tapering. To duplicate this effect, wrap the entire stem

26-10. *Stamen cluster.*

26-11. *Bend the flower's wire upward.*

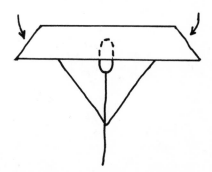

26-12. *Fold the long edge of the bud triangle over the cotton-tipped stem wire.*

wire once or twice with strips of tissue paper and glue. Continue wrapping from the tip to the base, this time increasing the number of wraps as you descend, so that the stem becomes thicker as you approach the base. The lower 4 inches of the stem should be thickest and should have the same diameter (that is, the final 4 inches should not be tapered).

Wrap the buds alternately along the stem wire with green floral tape, starting at the tapered end. The buds should be placed on the upper 5 inches of the stem. Next add the small flowers, wrapping with floral tape. All flowers must be attached so that the inside wire is upward. After the small flowers are on, wrap on all the large flowers. Finally, wrap the leaves on the stem. Place all the leaves near each other to form a rosette. Wrap to the end of the stem wire with green floral tape. Adjust the flowers so that the buds and small flowers extend outward at a slight angle. Make the large flowers extend outward at a greater angle.

CHAPTER 27

TULIP

*T*he tulip (of the family Lili-aceae) is a perennial bulb that has been cultivated for over a thousand years. It is of Oriental origin and symbolizes avowed love, or fame. The word *Tulip* is derived from the Turkish word for turban, which the flower closely resembles.

Materials
silk: white
cotton (optional)
starch
dyes: green, plus red or pastel
    color
cloth-covered wire to match the
    petals: #30
green cloth-covered wire: #30
6 commercial or handmade tulip
    stamen
stem wire: #16
thin strips of tissue paper
floral tape: green

Assembly
1 flower
2 leaves

    All the petals and leaves of the tulip are cut out of double-thickness fabric. Following the patterns given here (figs. 27-2 and 27-3), cut six pairs of petals out of starched silk, with the

27-1. *Tulip.*

91

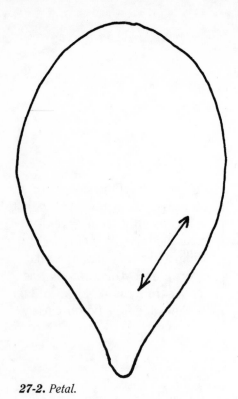

27-2. *Petal.*

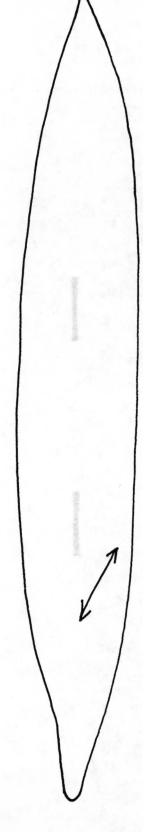

27-3. *Leaf.*

27-4. *Wrap the stamen cluster with tissue paper.*

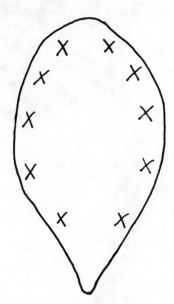

27-5. *Iron each petal at the Xs.*

fabric doubled so that you cut one pair at a time. Keep the bases of the petal pairs pinned as you cut them so they stay together symmetrically throughout the dyeing process. Cut the two leaf pairs out of cotton or silk and keep each pair of leaves pinned together.

Dye the petals red or any pastel color. The dye should penetrate both layers of the petal pairs. Dye the leaf pairs green in the same way. If you use cotton for the leaves, you might have to dye both sides, since the dye does not penetrate this fabric as easily.

Carefully glue cloth-covered wire (to match the petal color) inside each petal along the center, allowing about 2 inches of wire to extend below the base. To do this, apply glue along two opposite sides of the cloth-covered wire. Place the wire along the center of one petal, then take its mate and place it on top of the first petal so that it matches

exactly. Press along the wire with your finger. Do not apply glue directly to the silk in any other place; petals are glued together only at the wire.

Glue two lengths of green cloth-covered wire side by side along the center of the leaves in just the same way, with 2 inches of wire extending below the base. The doubled wire is used to make the long, bladelike leaves sturdier and less likely to droop.

You will need six commercial

or handmade tulip stamen. Baker's clay works well for tulip stamen if you form the dough in small cocoon shapes at the tips of 5-inch lengths of green cloth-covered wire #30. (See Chapter 2 for more information about making these kinds of stamen.) You may also make tulip stamen by wrapping the tips of six 5-inch lengths of green cloth-covered wire with green or yellow floral tape.

Attach the stamen cluster to the tip of a 12- to 18-inch length of #16 stem wire. Secure it to the stem wire by wrapping the cluster with thin strips of tissue paper and glue (fig. 27-4).

Iron each petal by pressing with a heated knife handle, as shown by the *X*s in figure 27-5. Iron the leaves by pressing with a heated knife edge next to one side of the wire.

Arrange all six petals around the base of the stamen with their ironed sides inward. Secure the petals to the stem wire by wrapping the base of each flower with thin strips of tissue paper and glue. To give the flower a natural appearance, the petals should overlap each other.

The stem of the tulip is rather thick. To obtain this effect, wrap all the way down the stem wire with thin strips of tissue paper and glue. Repeat this process once more to make the stem even thicker. Now start wrapping the stem wire below the flower with green floral tape. Add the two leaves about halfway down and continue wrapping with the tape to the end of the stem wire.

CHAPTER 28

ORIENTAL POPPY

*T*he Oriental poppy (of the genus *Papaver*) was long associated by the Romans with Morpheus, god of sleep and death. In flower language the poppy has a number of meanings, depending on the variety. It can mean evanescent pleasure or consolation or fantastic extravagance.

Materials
silk: white
rayon velvet
cotton (optional
starch
dyes: red or orange, black, green
green cloth-covered wire: #30
red or orange cloth-covered wire: #30
absorbent cotton
stem wire: #16, #30
24 commercial stamen: black
thin strips of tissue paper

Assembly
1 flower
2 leaves
velvet stem strip

Following the patterns given here (figs. 28-2 through 28-5), cut eight petals out of starched white silk and cut two leaves out of starched cotton, velvet, or silk. Cut one disc out of starched silk.

28-1. *Oriental poppy.*

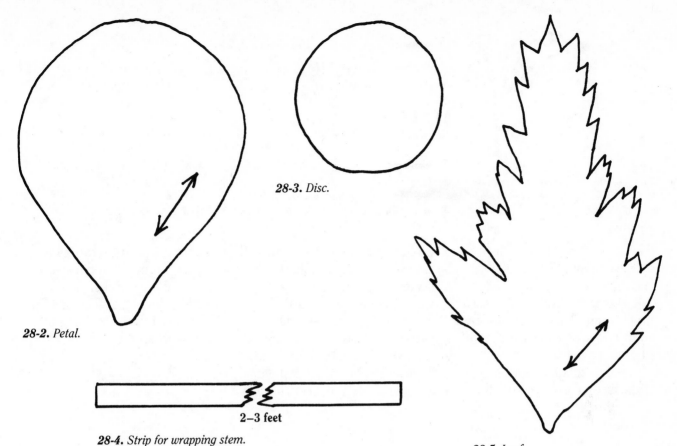

28-2. Petal.

28-3. Disc.

2–3 feet

28-4. Strip for wrapping stem.

28-5. Leaf.

28-6. Use an extra V-shaped wire to support each leaf.

28-7. Wrap the disc over the cotton ball.

Cut a narrow 2- to 3-foot strip of velvet for wrapping the stem.

Dye the petals red or orange. Deepen the color at the base or dye the area near the base black. Dye the leaves, the disc, and the stem fabric green. The green velvet wrapped around the stem wire gives the stem a realistic fuzzy look. You can fray the edges of the stem fabric a little for an even fuzzier look.

Glue green cloth-covered wire along the center and lower sides on the back of each leaf (fig. 28-6). Be sure to let about 2 inches of wire extend below the base. Glue red or orange cloth-covered wire along the center of each petal, allowing about 2 inches of wire to extend below the base. You can snip the edges of the petals so that they appear slightly serrated.

Wrap and glue absorbent cotton into a rounded shape (½ inch in diameter) at the end of a 12- to 18-inch length of #16 stem wire. Apply glue thinly on one surface of a disc and wrap it over the cotton, pinching it together below the cotton (fig. 28-7).

Gather about twenty-four black commercial stamen and twist them with a piece of #30 stem wire at their centers. Bend the stamen up. (See fig. 28-8.) Arrange the stamen to encircle the disc-covered cotton (fig. 28-9), bind them together, down about 3 inches, with thin strips of tissue paper and glue.

Iron each petal on the unwired side with a heated knife handle, as shown by the *X*s in figure 28-10. Or, instead of ironing the petals, you might wish to wrinkle the petals and then wave the edges, giving the

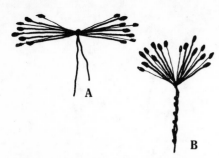

28-8. (A) *Tie the stamens at their centers.* (B) *Bend the stamens upward to form a cluster.*

28-9. *Arrange the stamen cluster around the disc-covered cotton.*

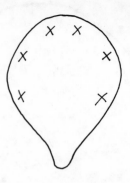

28-10. *Iron each petal at the Xs.*

flower a very professional look. (See "Wrinkling Petals" and "Waving Edges" in Chapter 2 for details of this technique.) Make a simple branching vein structure on the wired side of each leaf with a heated knife edge.

Apply a small amount of glue at the base of each petal on the wired side and arrange them around the stamen. (Shape the petals by curving their wires slightly so the petals turn inward.) The petals should overlap each other. Wrap the stem wire below the petals with the thin strip of velvet and glue for only about 3 inches. This will secure the petals to the stem wire. Continue wrapping with glue and the velvet strip. About halfway down the stem, add the leaves. Continue wrapping with the velvet strip to the end of the stem wire.

CHAPTER 29

ANEMONE

*T*he anemone (of the family Ranunculaceae) is commonly called a windflower. (*Anemos* is the Greek word for wind.) Anemones are quite fragile and short-lived and are often associated with sorrow and death. In Victorian flower language they can mean sickness or desertion.

Materials
silk: white, green (optional)
rayon velvet: white, green
cotton (optional)
starch
dye: green (optional)
green cloth-covered wire: #30
white cloth-covered wire: #30
stem wire: #16
absorbent cotton
15 commercial stamen: yellow
thin strips of tissue paper

Assembly
1 flower
1 bud
3 large leaves
8 small leaves
2 center discs
velvet stem strip

Following the patterns given here (figs. 29-2 through 29-7), cut six petals out of starched white silk. Use a combination of *A*

29-1. *Anemone.*

97

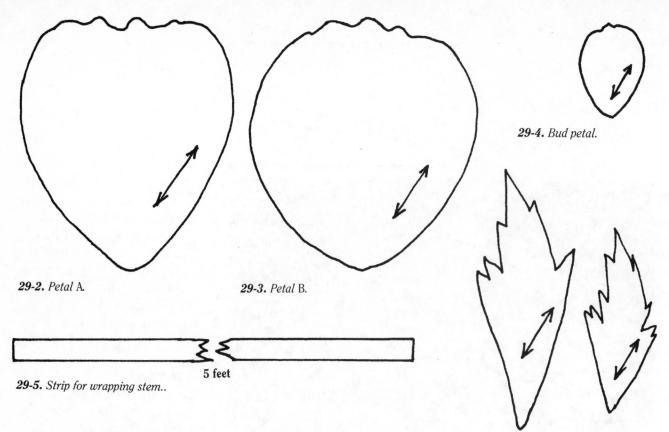

29-2. Petal A.

29-3. Petal B.

29-4. Bud petal.

5 feet

29-5. Strip for wrapping stem..

29-6. Large leaf.　　29-7. Small leaf.

29-8. Three-leaf group.

29-9. Two-leaf group.

petals and *B* petals. For instance, you could use two *A* petals and 4 *B* petals. Cut two discs out of green silk. Cut three large leaves and eight small leaves out of starched green silk or cotton. Cut four bud petals out of starched white velvet. The green velvet stem strip should be about 5 feet long.

Glue green cloth-covered wire along the center of each leaf, allowing 3 inches of wire to extend below the base. Glue white cloth-covered wire along the center of each petal and bud petal, allowing 2 inches of wire to extend below the base.

Iron the leaves with a heated knife edge on the wired side, showing a simple branching vein structure. Then group the leaves so that they are trifoliate (in groups of threes), with a large one in the middle and one small one on each side (fig. 29-8). Then take two small leaves and group them together (fig. 29-9). You

should have three groups of three leaves and one group of two leaves. Wrap their stems with thin strips of green velvet and glue. The green velvet strips give a fuzzy look that is characteristic of the stems of anemones.

Iron each petal on the unwired side with a heated knife handle, as shown by the *X*s in figure 29-10. Iron the bud petals also with a heated knife handle, but iron them on the wired side, as shown by the *X*s in figure 29-11. Instead of ironing the silk petals, you can shape them by wrinkling the petals and then waving their edges. This gives your anemone a realistic look. (See "Wrinkling Petals" and "Waving Edges" in Chapter 2 for details of this technique.)

Next make the center disc with the stamen. Take an 18-inch length of #16 stem wire and wrap its tip with absorbent cotton to form a bulge. Apply glue to the surface of a disc and wrap it over

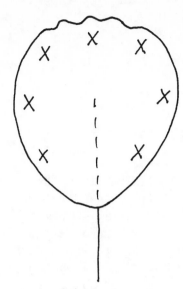

29-10. *Iron each petal at the Xs.*

29-13. *Pinch the edges of the disc around the base of the cotton ball.*

the absorbent cotton and pinch its base. (See figs. 29-12 and 29-13). Now take a group of about fifteen commercial yellow stamen and wrap them together at the center with some yellow cloth-covered wire #30 (fig. 29-14). Place the center of the stamen near the base of the disc-covered cotton, bend the stamen upward, and arrange them so that they surround the disc. Wrap the base

29-14. *Tie the stamens at their centers.*

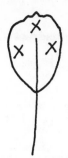

29-11. *Iron each bud petal at the Xs.*

of the stamen and down the stem wire a few inches with thin strips of tissue paper and glue (fig. 29-15).

To make the flower, place the six petals around the stamen, unwired sides inward. Secure the petals to the stem wire by wrapping their stems to the main stem wire with thin strips of tissue paper and glue. Then wrap below the flower and down the stem wire with green velvet strips and glue. Wrap down the stem only about 6 inches.

To make the bud, first take a 15-inch piece of #16 stem wire and make a ball of absorbent cotton at its tip. Glue the other disc over it, as you did for the flower, but do not place stamen around this disc. Arrange the four bud petals around the disc-covered cotton, wired sides inward. Wrap below the bud with strips of green velvet and glue (fig.

29-15. *Wrap the stamen cluster with tissue paper.*

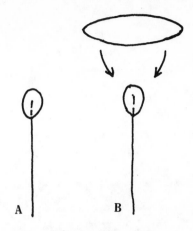

29-12. (A) *Wrap absorbent cotton on stem wire.* (B) *Glue the disc over the cotton.*

29-16). Wrap down the stem about 8 inches, then attach the group of two leaves to this stem as you wrap with the velvet strip and glue.

To assemble the finished flower, continue wrapping below the flower with green velvet strips and glue. Add the three groups of three leaves as you wrap. Then add the stem with the bud. Continue wrapping to the end of the main stem wire with green velvet strips and glue. Arrange the leaves so that they extend out from the stem at an angle. Bend the flower downward slightly to make it more visible. Then bend the bud's stem downward in a deep curving arch so that the bud droops.

29-16. *Bud.*

CHAPTER 30

FUCHSIA

30-1. *Fuchsia.*

*T*he fuchsia was first discovered growing in the West Indies in the 1800s. The genus *Fuchsia* was named after the German botanist Leonard Fuchs, who died in 1566. The fuchsia generally is a shrub and often grows in hedges or against a cottage wall. Today there are over 2,000 hybrid varieties.

Materials
silk: white
starch
dyes: pink, deep purple, green
pink cloth-covered wire: #30
16 commercial stamen: black
stem wire: #16, #18, #30
thin strips of tissue paper
white cloth-covered wire: #30
floral tape: yellow, green, pink
absorbent cotton

Assembly
2 flowers
1 bud
15 leaves
4 sets of sepals

These flowers call for patience and meticulous handwork. Following the patterns given here (figs. 30-2 through 30-5), cut eight petals out of starched white silk and dye them fuchsia (pink)

100

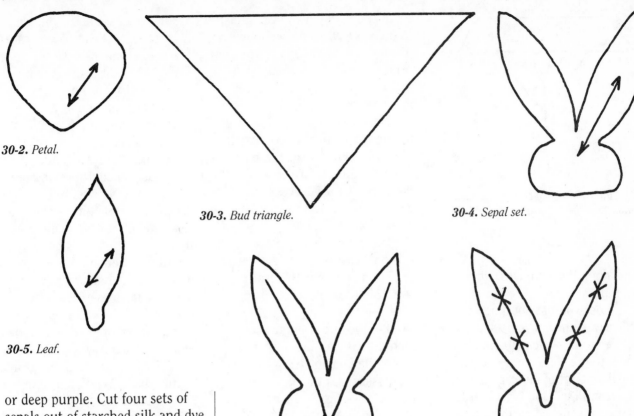

30-2. *Petal.*

30-3. *Bud triangle.*

30-4. *Sepal set.*

30-5. *Leaf.*

30-6. *Glue a* V-*shaped wire onto each sepal.*

30-7. *Iron each sepal set at the Xs.*

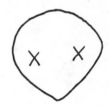

30-8. *Iron each petal at the Xs.*

or deep purple. Cut four sets of sepals out of starched silk and dye them pink. Cut fifteen leaves out of starched silk and dye them green. Cut out one silk bud triangle and dye it pink.

Glue pink cloth-covered wire to each sepal set in a V shape. Be sure the corner of the V extends partway into the base of the sepals (fig. 30-6). Do not glue wire to the petals or leaves.

Iron each sepal set with a heated knife handle on the wired side, as shown by the *X*s in figure 30-7. Iron each petal with a heated knife handle, as shown by the *X*s in figure 30-8.

Gather up about eight black stamen and cut off one end of each. With thin strips of tissue paper and glue, attach the stamen to the tip of an 18-inch length of #16 stem wire. To make the pistil, take a 5-inch length of white cloth-covered wire #30 and apply a tiny amount of glue to one tip. Wrap a ¾-inch length of yellow floral tape around this tip to form the stigma of the pistil.

Attach the pistil on the stem wire next to the stamen in the same manner as you did for the stamen. Wrap green floral tape over the tissue paper down only 1 inch (fig. 30-9).

Apply small amount of glue to the bases of four petals on the ironed sides. Attach the petals to the base of the stamen with ironed sides inward. The petals should overlap.

Now lightly apply glue on the wired side of a sepal base. Wrap the sepal base around half of the base of the flower. Take another set of sepals, apply glue, and wrap it around the other half of the flower. You will have four sepals (two sets) on each flower. Curve them gently by bending their wires. Wrap over the sepal base

30-9. *Stamen and pistil cluster.*

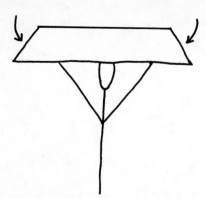

30-10. *Fold the long edge of the bud triangle over the cotton-tipped wire.*

and along the stem wire with pink floral tape.

Since you did not glue wire to the leaves, they have no stems. Therefore it is tricky to attach them to the stem wire. Apply a small amount of glue at the base of a leaf. Pinch and twist it at the base. The pinched part will form a small stem, which you can attach to the stem wire and secure with green floral tape. Add about three or four leaves as you wrap about 5 inches down the stem wire with green floral tape.

Now make another flower at the tip of a 5-inch length of #18 stem wire. Follow the same procedure you used for the first flower. Add a few leaves as you wrap down the stem wire with green floral tape.

Making the bud is easy. Take a 5-inch length of #18 stem wire and wrap one tip with absorbent cotton to form a cocoon shape. Fold down the long edge (the base) of the bud triangle about 1 inch. Slip the absorbent cotton under the fold and wrap the two corners around the base of the cotton. (See fig. 30-10.) Twist it at the base. Wrap stem wire #30 around the base of the bud and twist to secure. Cut off any excess fabric to eliminate bulkiness. Secure the bud at the base by wrapping it with thin strips of tissue paper and glue. Wrap down 2 inches along the stem. Wrap over the strips of tissue paper with green floral tape. Add a few leaves as you continue wrapping along the stem wire.

To assemble the completed flower, continue wrapping green floral tape along the stem wire of the first flower you made on #16 wire. Add the bud as you wrap with the tape, then add a few leaves, then the other flower. Continue wrapping down to the end of the stem wire with the tape. To arrange the fuchsias in a natural pose, bend each stem wire so that it arches downward.

CHAPTER 31

DOGWOOD

Dogwood (of the genus *Cornus*), sometimes called cornel, received its name from the Latin word for horn (*cornu*). Sacred to the Romans, it flourished in the classical world and allegedly supplied the wood for Christ's cross. It grows in the form of trees and shrubs, both evergreen and deciduous.

Materials
silk: white, green (optional)
cotton (optional)
starch
dye: green (optional)
marker: brown
white cloth-covered wire: #30
green cloth-covered wire: #30
stem wire: #16, #18, #30
absorbent cotton
floral tape: green, brown
commercial dogwood peps
thin strips of tissue paper

Assembly
4 blossoms
4 buds
11 leaves

Like the poinsettia, the flowers of the dogwood are actually the small central peps. The blossoms are actually bracts that surround the flowers.

31-1. Dogwood.

103

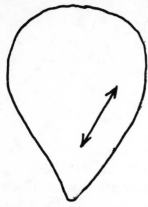

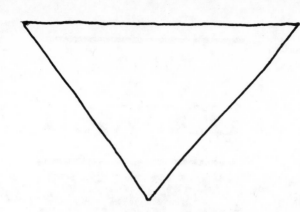

31-2. *Blossom or bract.*

31-3. *Bud triangle.*

31-4. *Leaf.*

31-5. *Iron each bract at the Xs and then along the vein lines.*

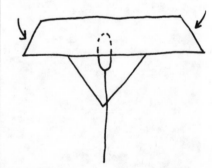

31-6. *Fold the long edge of the bud triangle over the cotton-tipped wire.*

Following the patterns given here (figs. 31–2 through 31–4), cut sixteen blossoms out of starched white silk. Cut eleven leaves out of starched green silk or cotton. Cut four buds out of white silk.

Dye the leaves green if you are using white silk. Do not dye the bracts. Instead, use a brown marker to make a small triangular mark near the rounded tip of each bract. (See fig. 31–1.)

Glue white cloth-covered wire along the center of each bract, allowing 2 inches of wire to extend below the base. Glue green cloth-covered wire along the center of each leaf, allowing 2 inches of wire to extend below the base.

Following figure 31–5, iron each bract at the *X*s on the unwired side with a heated knife handle. Then make the vein lines with a heated knife edge.

Iron the wired side of each leaf with a heated knife edge, showing a simple branching vein structure.

Make four buds on short (about 3-inch) lengths of #18 stem wire. Wrap the tip of each wire with absorbent cotton to form a small cocoon shape. Fold the long edge of a bud triangle down ½ inch and slip the cocoon

beneath this (fig. 31–6). Then bring the sides of the bud around and twist at the base of the cotton to form the bud. Wrap #30 stem wire around the base of the bud and twist to secure. Cut off any excess fabric below the bud base to eliminate bulkiness. Wrap below the bud and down the stem wire with green and then brown floral tape.

To assemble a flower, take an 8- to 10-inch length of #18 stem wire and attach the commercial dogwood peps to its tip with thin strips of tissue paper and glue. Now arrange four bracts around the peps, unwired sides upward, and secure them to the stem with thin strips of tissue paper and glue. The bracts should not overlap. Wrap the stem wire below the flower with brown floral tape and add two or three leaves as you wrap. Add a bud and a leaf—all buds should be in leaf crotches.

Make three more blossoms in just the same way; one blossom should have a short stem because it will be placed at the very tip of the main stem wire.

Now that you have four blossoms with buds and leaves attached, you are ready to assemble everything on the main stem. Take the short-stemmed

blossom and secure it to the tip of #16 stem wire with brown floral tape. Wrap downward with the tape, adding more blossoms as you go, until all are attached. Add any extra leaves as you continue wrapping to the end of the stem wire with the tape.

CHAPTER 32

FORGET-ME-NOT

*T*here are many stories about how the forget-me-not received its name, but one of the more romantic comes from a German legend. The story goes that a young woman, watching a lovely blue flower float down a river, sighed that she could not have it. Her lover jumped into the swift current to retrieve it and was swept away—but not before he tossed the flower to her and spoke his last words, "Forget me not." The forget-me-not (of the genus *Myosotis*) is popular as a border plant and is often used in cut-flower arrangements.

Materials
silk: white or blue, green
      (optional)
starch
dyes: green, blue (both optional)
yellow cloth-covered wire: #30
floral tape: green
stem wire: #18, #20

Assembly
18 flowers
18 calyxes
14 leaves

Instead of dyeing each little flower, it is much easier to cut eighteen petal sets from starched blue silk. Or cut an 8-inch square

32-1. Forget-me-not.

32-2. *Petal set.*

32-3. *Calyx.*

32-4. *Leaf.*

32-5. *Iron each petal set at the Xs.*

32-6. *Flower center.*

32-7. *Leaf cluster.*

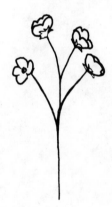

32-8. *Flower cluster.*

of white silk, dye it sky blue, and after it dries, cut out the eighteen petals. Cut sixteen leaves and eighteen calyxes from starched green silk. Follow the patterns given here (figs. 32-2 through 32-4).

Iron the petals with a heated knife handle, as shown by the *X*s in figure 32-5. Iron the leaves with a heated knife edge, making one longitudinal crease down the center. It is not necessary to wire the leaves.

Make the flower centers. Take a 4-inch length of yellow cloth-covered wire and make a small circle by wrapping the tip twice around the tip of an awl, or use needlenosed pliers to do this. (See fig. 32-6.) Make eighteen of these.

Pierce the center of a petal set with an awl to make a small hole. Apply a small amount of glue around the hole on the ironed side. Slip the end of the yellow cloth-covered wire through the hole so that the circular end rests on the glue. Apply a small amount of glue to the base of a calyx and wrap it below the flower. Wrap below the flower and down its thin yellow stem with thin strips of green floral tape. (Cut a length of green floral

tape in half lengthwise to eliminate bulkiness along the stem.) Make eighteen of these flowers.

To make a leaf cluster, of seven leaves take a 6-inch length of stem wire #20 and attach a leaf to its tip. There is no wire on the leaf, so you have to secure each leaf to the wire by wrapping its base with thin strips of green floral tape. Attach a few more leaves in the same way as you wrap the floral tape down the length of the wire. (See fig. 32-7.) Make another leaf cluster the same way.

Now you are ready to assemble the finished flowers. Take four or five flowers and attach them to the tip of a 12-inch length of #18 stem wire with green floral tape. The flowers should be attached near each other—not at exactly the same place. (See fig. 32-8.) Now take three 5-inch lengths of #18 wire and follow the same procedure, wrapping four or five flowers near their tips. Attach the short stem wires along the main stem at intervals as you wrap with green floral tape. When all of the flowers are on, wrap on the leaf clusters. Wrap to the end of the main stem with green floral tape.

CHAPTER 33

LILAC

*T*he lilac (of the genus *Syringa*) generally grows as a shrub. For centuries the color purple has been associated with death, so the lilac, being primarily purple and violet, has come to have the same significance. In Victorian flower language, the white lilac can mean purity or modesty; the purple lilac can signify the first emotions of love.

Materials
silk: white, green (optional)
cotton (optional)
starch
dyes: pink or lavender, green
    (optional)
green cloth-covered wire: #30
floral tape: green, yellow
stem wire: #16, #24
absorbent cotton
commercial peps (optional)

Assembly
15 flowers
5 buds
4 leaves

Following the patterns given here (figs. 33-2 through 33-4), cut fifteen petal sets out of starched white silk. Cut five bud triangles out of white silk. Cut

33-1. Lilac.

107

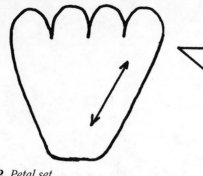

33-2. *Petal set.*

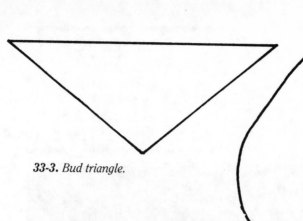

33-3. *Bud triangle.*

33-4. *Leaf.*

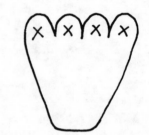

33-5. *Iron each petal set at the Xs.*

33-6. *Stamen.*

33-7. *Glue the cylindrical petal set around the stamens and wrap tape around its base and down the stem wire.*

four leaves out of starched green silk or cotton.

Dye the tips of the petal sets dusty pink or lavender, leaving the rest white. If you are using white fabric, dye the leaves green. Dye the bud triangles pale dusty pink or lavender. Leave some of the bud fabric white as a natural accent.

Glue green cloth-covered wire along the center of each leaf, allowing 4 inches of wire to extend below the base. Then wrap each leaf stem with green floral tape.

Iron each leaf on the wired side with a heated knife edge, showing a simple branching vein structure. Iron the tips of the petal sets with a heated knife handle, as shown by the *X*s in figure 33-5. If you can find a very small round metal object, such as the rounded end of a nut pick handle, that can be heated safely, try ironing the flower tips with it.

Next make the stamen. Cut fifteen four-inch lengths of #24 stem wire and wrap only their tips with yellow floral tape to form a bulge. Then cut the yellow tape in half lengthwise to make narrower strips. Wrap below the yellow bulge with a thin strip of the tape for about 1 inch. (See fig. 33-6.) Make fifteen of these stamen.

To make one flower, apply glue to one side edge of a petal set and form it into a cylinder by overlapping the side edges. The flower tips should radiate outward. Apply a small amount of glue around the base of the flower on the inside of the cylinder. Insert a stamen. Pinch the base of the flower around the base of the stamen and wrap the base of the flower and down the stem with thin strips of green floral tape. (Make these thin strips of green floral tape by cutting the tape in half lengthwise to eliminate bulkiness.) (See fig. 33-7.) Make fifteen of these flowers.

To make a bud, wrap the tip of a 4-inch length of #24 stem wire with absorbent cotton to form a bulge the size of a peppercorn. Fold the long edge (the base) of a bud triangle down ½ inch and slip the cotton below the fold (fig. 33-8). Bring the corners of the triangle around and twist the fabric at the base of the bud. Wrap below the bud and down the stem with thin strips of green floral tape. Make five of these buds.

Instead of making silk buds, you may wish to use commercial bud peps. Or you can make these small buds out of baker's clay (see "Further Techniques" in Chapter 2). Paint the baker's clay bud with white acrylic paint, and when dry, dab pink acrylic paint on its tip.

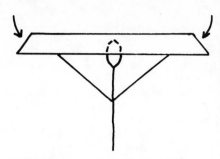

33-8. Fold the long edge of the bud triangle over the cotton-tipped wire.

To assemble the finished flower, take an 18-inch length of #16 stem wire. Attach a bud to its tip and secure it with green floral tape. Add the other buds to the stem wire at ½-inch intervals as you wrap with green floral tape. Then add the flowers, also at ½-inch intervals, until you have wrapped them all to the stem. Wrap the leaf stems onto the main stem below the flowers. Each leaf should have about 2 or 3 inches of its stem showing. Wrap to the end of the main stem wire with green floral tape. For a natural look, bend the flower stems outward slightly. The lilac flowers should appear clustered.

33-9. Pep made from baker's clay.

CHAPTER 34

CORNFLOWER

34-1. *Cornflower.*

Sometimes called the bluebottle for its intense royal blue color, the cornflower (of the genus *Centaurea*) is commonly seen growing in fields. In Victorian flower language, the cornflower signifies delicacy.

Materials
silk: white, green (optional)
starch
dyes: blue, green (optional)
green cloth-covered wire: #30
8 commercial stamen: black or
    white
stem wire: #20
floral tape: green

Assembly
4 flowers
4 leaves

Following the patterns given here (figs. 34-2 and 34-3), cut eight petal circles out of starched white silk and cut four leaves out of starched white or green silk.

Dye the petal circles blue. You may wish to leave the centers of the circles white. If you are using white fabric, dye the leaves green.

Glue green cloth-covered wire along the center of each leaf. Be sure to allow about 2 inches of wire to extend below the base.

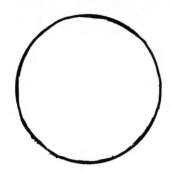

34-2. Petal circle.

34-3. Leaf.

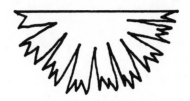

34-4. Make jagged snips along the edges of each petal semicircle.

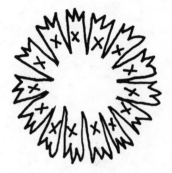

34-5. Iron each petal circle at the Xs.

34-6. Stamen cluster.

34-7. Insert the stamens through two glued petal circles. One circle bends upward, the other bends downward.

Fold a petal circle in half to form a semicircle. With small, sharp scissors, make jagged snips along the edge (fig. 34-4). Cut all the petal circles in this manner.

Iron the petals with a heated knife handle, as shown by the *X*s in figure 34-5.

To make a stamen cluster, take two commercial stamen and cut them in half to make four. Attach the four stamen to the tip of a 4-inch length of #20 stem wire with thin strips of green floral tape (fig. 34-6). (To make these thin strips of tape, cut a short piece in half lengthwise to eliminate bulkiness.)

Next make the flowers. Place a small amount of glue in the center of the unironed side of one petal circle. Place the unironed side of another petal circle on top of it. One petal circle will be curved upward and the other downward. Pierce the center of the two glued petal circles with an awl. Apply glue around the hole on one side. Insert a stamen cluster through the hole on the glued side. Slip the petal circles

up and secure them at the base of the stamen cluster. Wrap below the flower and down its stem with thin strips of green floral tape. (See fig. 34-7.)

To assemble the cornflower stalk, take a 12-inch length of #20 stem wire and wrap one flower to its tip with green floral tape. Add one leaf as you wrap. Wrap down the stem another 2 inches, then add another flower and leaf. Continue wrapping and adding flowers and leaves. Wrap to the end of the stem wire with the tape.

CHAPTER 35

BUTTERCUP

*T*he buttercup (of the genus *Ranunculus*), sometimes called a crowfoot, often grows in meadows or other marshy areas. Worldwide, there are nearly 300 species of buttercup. In flower language, the buttercup can mean cheerfulness or childishness.

Materials

silk: white or yellow and green
starch
dyes: green, yellow (both
    optional)
green cloth-covered wire: #30
stem wire: #20
floral tape: yellow, green

Assembly

3 flowers
3 calyxes
3 leaves
3 stamen strips

If you can, use yellow and green starched silk to make the buttercup in order to avoid the dyeing step. If these colors are not available, dye the petal sets and stamen yellow and the leaves and calyxes green.

Following the patterns given here (figs. 35-2 through 35-5), cut six petal sets and three

35-1. *Buttercup.*

112

35-2. *Petal set.*

35-3. *Calyx.*

35-4. *Stamen strip.*

stamen strips out of starched yellow silk. Cut three leaves and three calyxes out of starched green silk.

Glue green cloth-covered wire along the center of each leaf, allowing about 2 inches of wire to extend below the base.

Iron each leaf on the wired side with one lengthwise stroke, using a heated knife edge right next to the wire. Iron the petal sets and calyxes with a heated knife handle, as shown by the *X*s in figures 35-6 and 35-7. Make deep slits along the top edge of a stamen strip and then iron the strip, as shown by the *X*s in figure 35-8.

Take a 12-inch length of #20 stem wire, wrap ½ inch of its tip with yellow floral tape, and then bend this tip into a small hook. Apply glue all along the base of a stamen strip on the ironed side. Slip the hook through one of the slits at the end of the stamen strip (fig. 35-9) and roll it up to make a tight stamen cluster. Take two shorter lengths of #20 stem wire (about 8 inches each) and

follow the same procedure, so that you have three stamen clusters for the three flowers.

With an awl, pierce the centers of the ironed sides of two petal sets and one calyx. Apply glue around the holes on the ironed sides of these three pieces.

35-5. *Leaf.*

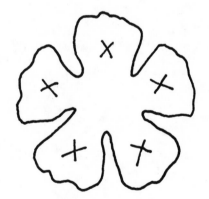

35-6. *Iron each petal set at the Xs.*

35-7. *Iron each calyx at the Xs.*

35-8. *Iron each stamen strip at the Xs after making deep slits along the top edge.*

The Flowers 113

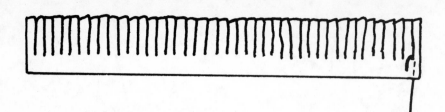

35-9. *Hook wire into the last slit on the stamen strip.*

Now slip the stem wire of one stamen cluster through the hole of a petal set and slide the petal set up. Secure the petal set just below the stamen cluster. Now take another petal set and slide it up below the first petal set, with alternate petal lobes. Next take the calyx and slide it up and secure it below the petal sets.

Wrap below the flower and down the stem several inches with green floral tape. Make two more flowers in just the same way.

To assemble the finished flower, take the flower on the longest stem and continue wrapping down the stem with green floral tape. After you are a little past halfway down the stem, add the other two flowers and the leaves. Continue wrapping to the end of the stem wire with the tape.

CHAPTER 36

DAY LILY AND TIGER LILY

The day lily (of the genus *Hemerocallis—hemera* from the Greek word meaning day and *kalos* meaning beautiful) is native to the Orient and some parts of southern Europe. Today modern hybrids grow everywhere. These modern lilies will last longer than their original varieties, which were short-lived, as the name day lily implies.

Materials

silk: green, plus wide variety of petal colors (optional)
cotton (optional)
starch
dyes: green, plus wide variety of petal colors (optional)
cloth-covered wire to match the petals: #30
green cloth-covered wire: #30
commercial or handmade stamen: black, white, or yellow
stem wire: #16, #18
thin strips of tissue paper
floral tape: green
marker: brown (to make tiger lily from day lily)

Assembly

1 flower
1 bud
2 large leaves
2 small leaves

36-1. Tiger lily (made from day lily patterns).

115

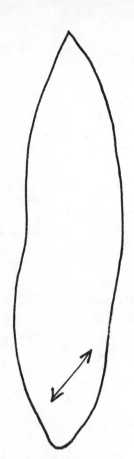

36-2. *Flower petal.*

36-3. *Bud petal.*

36-4. *Small leaf.*

36-5. *Large leaf.*

Following the patterns given here (figs. 36-2 through 36-5), cut six flower petals and three bud petals out of starched silk. Cut two small leaves and two large ones out of starched silk or cotton.

There are many lily colors to choose from. You can dye the petals pink, red, or yellow, or leave them white. An attractive effect comes from leaving the base of each petal white while dyeing the rest. Dye the leaves green.

Glue cloth-covered wire (to match the petals) along the center of each petal, including each bud petal, allowing about 2 inches of wire to extend below the base. Glue green cloth-covered wire along the center of each leaf,

allowing 2 inches of wire to extend below the base.

Cut the ends off of six commercial stamen and cluster them at the tip of a 12-inch length of #16 stem wire. Secure them to the stem wire with thin strips of tissue paper and glue.

To make your own stamen, try forming baker's clay into the shape of lily stamen at the tips of 5-inch lengths of green cloth-covered wire. (See "Further Techniques" in Chapter 2.) You can also make stamen by wrapping green or yellow floral tape around the tip of the wire (fig. 36-6).

36-6. *Handmade stamens.*

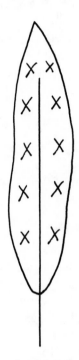

36-7. *Iron each petal at the Xs.*

Iron all the petals with a heated knife handle on the wired side, as shown by *X*s in figure 36-7. Iron the leaves with a heated knife edge by making a crease along the wire on the wired side.

To make the flower, arrange all six petals around the stamen cluster, unwired side up. Secure the petals to the stem wire at the base of the flower with thin strips of tissue paper and glue. Wrap over the tissue paper and down the stem for about 5 inches with green floral tape. Curve the petals downward slightly. Add a small leaf and wrap down 2 more inches with floral tape.

To make the bud, cluster three small stamen (or use none) at the tip of a 5-inch length of #18 stem wire. Secure the stamen to the stem wire with thin strips of tissue paper and glue. Now place the three small bud petals around the stamen, wired sides inward. These petals should extend upward and partially conceal the stamen. Secure the bud petals to the stem wire by wrapping the base of the bud with thin strips of tissue paper and glue. Wrap over the tissue paper with green floral tape, add a small leaf, and continue wrapping.

To assemble the completed flower, continue wrapping the stem wire of the flower with green floral tape. Add the bud as you wrap. When you are about halfway down the stem wire, add the two large leaves and continue wrapping with floral tape to the end of the stem wire.

Tiger Lily Assembly

It is very easy to convert the day lily into a charming tiger lily. You only need to make small dots on each petal with a brown marker, starting near the base of a petal and working toward the tip, filling about three-quarters of the length of the petal. The bud petals can also be marked, as shown in figure 36–1. Tiger lilies look especially appropriate in yellow or orange. You might also wish to make a smaller version of the lily by scaling down the pattern. These smaller lilies are very attractive when grouped three to a stem.

CHAPTER 37

BLACK-EYED SUSAN

37-1. *Black-eyed Susan.*

*T*he Black-eyed Susan (of the genus *Rudbeckia* in the family Compositae) is sometimes called a coneflower because of the small cone at the center of the blossom. The genus *Rudbeckia* comprises fewer than thirty species.

Materials
silk: yellow, brown, green (or use
    white)
cotton (optional)
rayon velvet
starch
dyes: yellow, brown, green (all
    optional)
green cloth-covered wire: #30
yellow cloth-covered wire: #30
thread: yellow
stem wire: #16
thin strips of tissue paper
absorbent cotton
floral tape: green

Assembly
1 flower
center cone
1 calyx
2 small leaves
2 large leaves

Following the patterns given here (figs. 37-2 through 37-7), cut two petal strips out of starched yellow silk. Cut one

37-2. *Petal strip.*

37-3. *Calyx.*

37-4. *Inner cone.*

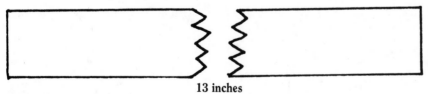

13 inches

37-5. *Outer cone strip.*

inner cone out of starched brown silk and one outer cone out of starched brown-rayon velvet. Cut two small leaves, two large ones, and one calyx out of starched green silk or cotton. If you cannot obtain these fabric colors,

start with white fabric and dye the pieces the appropriate colors.

Glue green cloth-covered wire along the center of each leaf, allowing about 2 inches of wire to extend below the base.

Fold each petal strip in half

from right to left to show half its length. With small, sharp scissors, make deep slits and cut the petals to give their tips a ragged look (fig. 37-8). Unfold each petal strip. If you wish, you can dye the center of each petal lobe brown. (See fig. 37-9 for dyeing pattern.) Glue yellow cloth-covered wire along each petal, allowing 1 inch to extend below the base (fig. 37-10). With yellow thread, sew wide running stitches along the base of each petal strip. Do not knot or finish off.

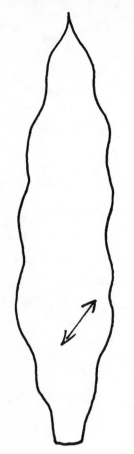

37-6. *Large leaf.*

37-7. *Small leaf.*

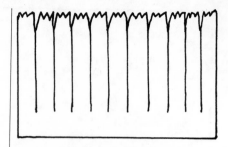

37-8. *Fold the petal strip in half and make slits to form the individual petals. Snip the tips to make a ragged edge.*

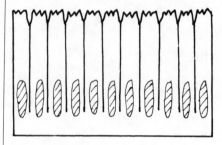

37-9. *Dye each petal at the lozenge-shaped mark.*

Iron the petals with a heated knife handle on the wired side, as shown by the *X*s in figure 37-10. Iron the calyx with a heated knife handle, as shown by the *X*s in figure 37-11.

Next make the cone. Take the inner cone, pinch its center, and wrap cloth-covered wire around it

to gather, as shown in figure 37-12. Then attach the wire to a 12-inch length of #16 stem wire by wrapping with thin strips of tissue paper and glue, as shown in figure 37-13. Wrap the pinched part with absorbent cotton to form a bulge about the size of a marble, as shown in figure 37-14. Now bring the silk down over the cotton to cover the bulge. Twist it at the base and wrap it with cloth-covered wire to secure it, as shown in figure 37-15. Wrap below this small bulge with absorbent cotton to

form a large, olive-sized bulge. This olive-sized bulge will cover both the excess silk and the wire below the small top bulge. Wrap the larger bulge with thin strips of tissue paper and glue, as shown in figure 37-16. Now take the velvet outer cone strip and make deep slits along its top edges. Iron the strip on the back side with a heated knife handle, as shown by the *X*s in figure 37-17. Apply glue along the base of the strip on the ironed side. Wrap the outer cone strip around the olive-sized bulge

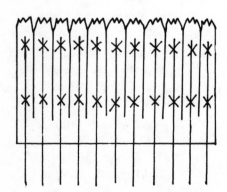

37-10. *Iron the petals at the Xs.*

37-11. *Iron the calyx at the Xs.*

37-12. *Pinch the inner cone at its center and wrap it with wire.*

37-13. *Attach the pinched cone to a 12-inch length of #16 stem wire.*

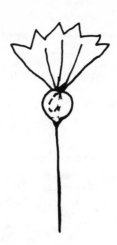

37-14. *Wrap cotton below the inner cone.*

37-15. *Pull the inner cone down over the cotton and secure it with wire.*

37-16. *Add cotton below the small bulge to make a larger bulge and cover it with tissue paper and glue.*

37-17. *Slit the velvet outer cone strip and iron it at the Xs.*

37-18. *Wrap the cone strip spirally so that it covers the cotton and some of the upper silk ball.*

spirally, as shown in figure 37-18. You may need to trim some of the fringe near the inner cone to make sure it is not obscured.

Now you are ready to assemble the flower. Apply glue along the base of the petal strip on the unwired side and pull the thread to gather the petal strip. Wrap the petal strip around the base of the cone. The edges should overlap only slightly. Apply the second petal strip below the first in the same way. Pierce the center of the calyx with an awl on the unironed side and apply glue around the hole on the unironed side. Slip the flower's stem through this hole on the unironed side and slide the calyx up to secure it below the flower. The petals and the calyx sepals should droop slightly. Wrap below the flower and down the stem with green floral tape. Add the two small leaves, then the two large leaves as you wrap to the end of the stem wire with the tape.

CHAPTER 38

ORIENTAL MORNING GLORY

*T*he morning glory (of the family Convolvulaceae) is sometimes called bindweed because its clinging, vinelike growth is almost impossible to untangle. Nevertheless, it makes a beautiful bouquet; the hand-made flower actually works better in bouquets than the real flower does, since the real flower closes up tightly soon after being picked.

Materials
silk: white
satin (optional)
starch
dyes: pink or purple or blue,
    green
green cloth-covered wire: #30
8 commercial stamen: white
thin strips of tissue paper
stem wire: #16, #18
absorbent cotton
floral tape: green

Assembly
1 flower
3 small leaves
2 large leaves
1 petal support
2 calyxes
1 bud
1 tendril

Following the patterns given here (figs. 38-2 through 38-7),

38-1. *Oriental morning glory.*

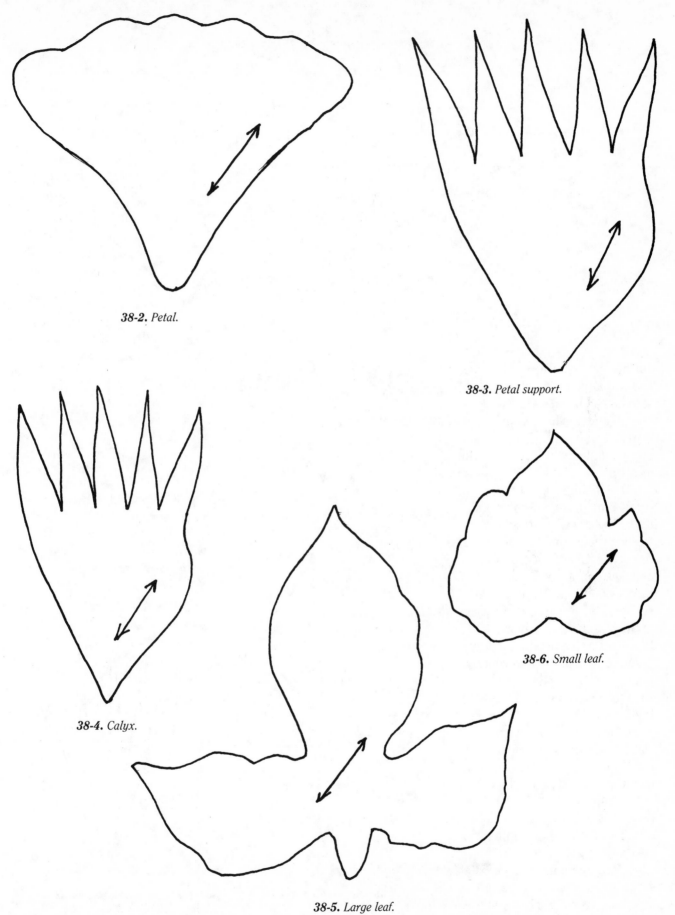

38-2. *Petal.*

38-3. *Petal support.*

38-4. *Calyx.*

38-6. *Small leaf.*

38-5. *Large leaf.*

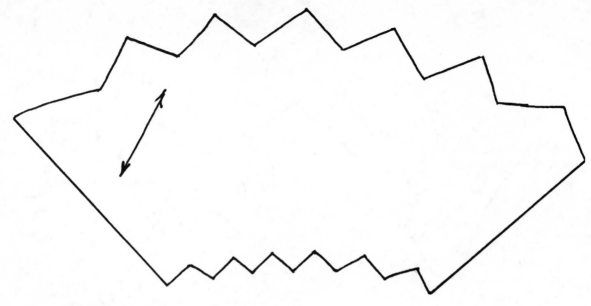

38-7. *Bud.*

cut five petals, three small leaves, and two large ones out of starched white silk. Cut two calyxes and one bud out of starched white silk. Cut one petal support out of starched white silk or satin.

Dye the top edges of the petals pink, purple, or blue and leave the base white (fig. 38-8). Deepen the color near the tips of the petals. Dye the leaves green and deepen the color in the center of each leaf. Dye the petal support pale green. Dye the apex of the bud the same color as the top edges of the petals, and leave the wide base of the bud white. Dye the calyxes green. You may wish to accent the sepal tips with the petal color.

Glue three pieces of green cloth-covered wire on each large leaf. Cut the ends of the wires different lengths to relieve bulkiness in the stem. (See fig. 38-9.) Wire each small leaf with green cloth-covered wire, as shown in figure 38-10. Glue green cloth-covered wire along the fingers of the petal support and down to its base, as shown in figure 38-11. If you use

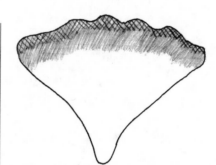

38-8. *Dye the shaded area of each petal and leave the rest white.*

38-10. *The small leaf needs only one central support wire.*

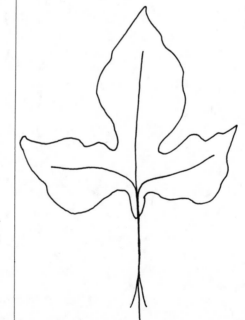

38-9. *Use three wires to support the large leaf.*

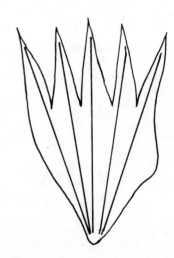

38-11. *Wire the petal support in a fanlike pattern.*

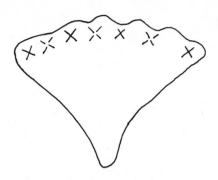

38-12. *Iron each petal at the Xs.*

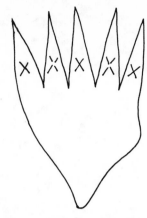

38-13. *Iron the calyx at the Xs.*

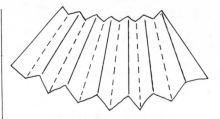

38-14. *Iron the bud on both sides so that it has accordion folds.*

satin, be sure to glue the wire to the back side of the fabric.

Use a heated knife edge to iron the veins of the leaves on the wired sides to show a compound branching vein structure. Iron the top edges of the petals with a heated knife handle, as shown by the *X*s in figure 38-12. Iron the sepals of the calyx with a heated knife handle, as shown by the *X*s in figure 38-13.

Iron the bud very carefully. Place the bud flat on the foam pad with the narrower tip upward. Start ironing with a heated knife edge from the first "peak" at the apex to the first "valley" at the base. Go to the next peak and repeat ironing every peak and valley. Then turn the bud over on the other side and iron from the valleys to the peaks, moving again from top to bottom. See fig. 38-14. The bud should then look like it has accordion folds, as shown in figure 38-14.

Next make the stamen. Cut off one end of a cluster of eight commercial stamen. Wrap these with thin strips of tissue paper and glue to the end of an 18-inch length of #16 stem wire. Continue wrapping with tissue paper until there is a slight bulge (fig. 38-15).

To make a flower, apply glue with a toothpick along the edge of a finger of the petal support, on the same side as the wires. Carefully glue the ironed sides of a petal to the sides of the finger on the petal support (fig. 38-16). The petal might bulge slightly in the middle. Apply glue to the side of the next finger on the petal support and glue on the next petal as you glued the first. Then glue the edge of the second petal to the edge of the first, allowing about ⅛-inch overlap. Continue until you have applied all the petals to the petal support. When the last petal is glued on, roll and glue the petal support into a cone, wired side out. Glue the side of the last petal to the side of the first petal. The petals should now flare like a trumpet (fig. 38-17).

Take the stamen and apply a small amount of glue at the base of the bulge. Insert the stem wire down inside the petal trumpet. (See fig. 38-18.) Apply a small amount of glue to the sides of the calyx base and wrap it around the trumpet of the flower. Secure the base of the calyx to the stem wire by wrapping below the calyx with green floral tape for about 1 inch.

To make the bud, first cut a

38-15. *Stamen cluster.*

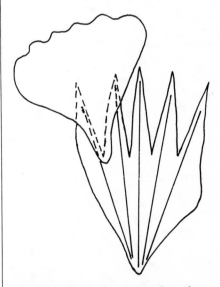

38-16. *Carefully glue the petals to the petal support, making allowances for minor adjustments.*

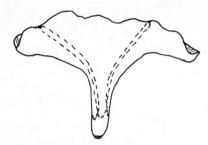

38-17. *When all the petals are glued to the petal support, they should flare out like the end of a trumpet.*

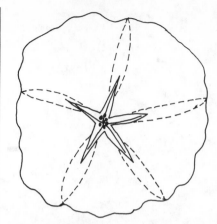

38-18. *Top view, looking into the trumpet mouth, showing the overlapping petals, the petal support, and the stamens.*

38-19. *Finished bud with calyx.*

6-inch length of #18 stem wire. Wrap small pieces of absorbent cotton around the tip of the stem wire to form a 2-inch-long cocoon shape. Glue the edges of the bud together in a cone shape. Apply small amounts of glue to the inside of the bud cone on the "peaks" at the top and at the bottom. Pinch together the peaks at the apex of the bud cone and place the cone over the absorbent cotton. Gather the peaks at the bottom and secure them to the stem wire below the absorbent

cotton. Hold the bud at the base with one hand and twist it at the top with the other hand. Wrap more absorbent cotton right below the bud to make a 1½-inch-long bulge. Apply a thin smear of glue along the base of the calyx and wrap it around the absorbent cotton. (See fig. 38-19.) Wrap down the stem wire

with green floral tape for about 1 inch. Wrap on the small leaves (no stem wire should be showing), with the unwired side of each leaf facing the main stem wire. Make a tendril by wrapping a 10-inch length of green cloth-covered wire spirally on an awl. Add the tendril while wrapping the main stem wire with green floral tape. Continue to wrap the flower's stem wire with the tape while adding the bud and the large leaves. Wrap the floral tape to the end of the stem wire.

CHAPTER 39

WILD MORNING GLORY

*T*he wild morning glory grows in abundance in vacant lots and along small streams and creeks. It grows in such profusion that its tangled vines often smother other plants. Its delicate blue blossoms set against its mass of green leaves produce a beautiful arrangement.

Materials

silk: white
cotton (optional)
starch
dyes: light blue, dark blue, green
12 to 16 commercial stamen:
    white
stem wire: #16, #18
thin strips of tissue paper
absorbent cotton
floral tape: green

Assembly

4 flowers
4 calyxes
2 small leaves
2 large leaves

Following the patterns given here (figs. 39-2 through 39-5), cut four petal circles out of starched white silk, then cut two small and two large leaves and four calyxes out of starched silk or cotton.

39-1. *Wild morning glory.*

39-2. *Petal circle.*

39-4. *Small leaf.*

39-3. *Calyx.*

39-5. *Large leaf.*

39-6. *Use an extra piece of wire to support the leaf.*

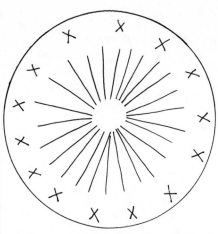

39-7. *Iron each petal circle at the Xs, and the use a knife edge to make a pattern of creases radiating from the center.*

39-8. *Iron the calyx at the Xs.*

Dye the petals blue, leaving the centers white. Deepen the outer edges of the petals with a darker blue. Dye the leaves and calyxes green.

Glue green cloth-covered wire along each lobe of the leaves, allowing 2 inches of wire to extend below the base of each leaf (fig. 39-6). Iron each leaf with a heated knife edge on the wired side, showing a simple branching vein structure on each leaf lobe.

Iron the petal circles with a heated knife handle, as shown by the *X*s in figure 39-7. Then iron the circles with a heated knife

edge, showing several creases radiating out from the center. Iron the calyx with a heated knife handle, as shown by the *X*s in figure 39-8.

Cut four deep slits in each petal circle, as shown in figure 39-9. Apply glue next to the slits and glue the edges so they overlap slightly. Then scallop the circumference of the circle with scissors, as shown in figure 39-10.

Make four stamen clusters. Make the first one at the tip of a 12-inch length of #16 stem wire. Take three or four commercial

stamen and cut off one end of each. Wrap them at the tip of the wire with thin strips of tissue paper and glue. Then make three more of these stamen clusters at the tips of 5-inch lengths of #18 stem wire.

Pierce the center of the concave side of a petal with an awl. Apply a small amount of glue around the hole on the concave side. Slip the stamen cluster through the hole on the glued side and slide the petal up and around the stamen. Secure it by pinching it below the stamen. Wrap below the flower with

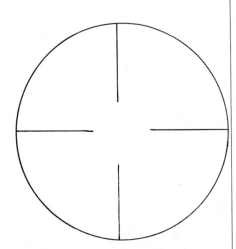

39-9. *Cut four deep slits in each petal circle.*

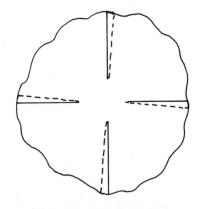

39-10. *Overlap and glue the edges of the slits, then scallop the circumference of the petal with scissors.*

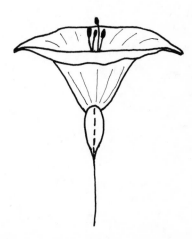

39-11. *Wrap absorbent cotton below the flower before attaching the calyx.*

absorbent cotton to form a cocoon shape about 1 inch long. (See fig. 39-11.) Apply glue to the base of the calyx and carefully wrap it around the absorbent cotton. Wrap below the calyx with green floral tape and down the stem a few inches.

Take a 6-inch length of #18 stem wire and attach the two small leaves to it. Make a tendril by wrapping green cloth-covered wire spirally around an awl. Attach the tendril near the small leaves.

To assemble the finished flower, continue wrapping below the flower on the main stem with green floral tape. Add the three other flowers, the small leaves with the tendril, then the two large leaves as you continue wrapping to the end of the stem wire with the tape.

CHAPTER 40

STEPHANOTIS

*T*he stephanotis (of the family Asclepiadaceae, which also includes the milkweed) is a very fragrant flower sometimes known as Madagascar jasmine. Stephanotis is often used to fill out wedding bouquets or boutonnieres.

Materials
silk: white, green (optional)
4-inch-wide satin ribbon: green (optional)
starch
dye: green (optional)
green cloth-covered wire: #30
stem wire: #18, #20
8 commercial stamen: white
thin strips of tissue paper
floral tape: green

Assembly
8 flowers
8 calyxes
4 leaves

Following the patterns given (figs. 40-2 through 40-4), cut eight petals out of starched white silk. Cut eight calyxes and four leaves out of starched green silk or green satin ribbon.

If you can find only white silk or white satin ribbon, dye the leaves green.

40-1. Stephanotis.

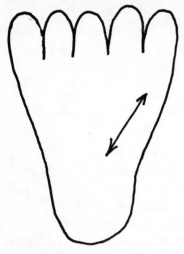

40-2. *Petal.*

40-3. *Calyx.*

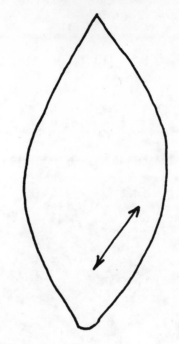

40-4. *Leaf.*

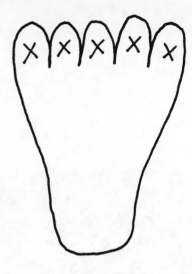

40-5. *Iron each petal at the Xs.*

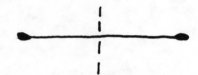

40-6. *Cut the stamens in half.*

40-7. *Attach two stamen halves to 5-inch lengths of stem wire.*

Glue green cloth-covered wire along the center of each leaf, allowing 2 inches of wire to extend below the base.

Iron the leaves on the wired side with a heated knife edge, showing a simple branching vein structure. Iron the tips of the petals with a heated knife handle, as shown by the *X*s in figure 40-5.

Take eight 5-inch lengths of #20 stem wire. Cut the eight stamen in half (fig. 40-6). Use two of these halves to attach to the tip of each #20 wire with thin strips of tissue paper and glue (fig. 40-7).

To make one flower, take a petal and apply glue thinly along its side edge on the ironed side. Carefully form the petal into a cylinder by gluing the side edges together. This job is easier if you start from the base of the flower as you glue. Now apply a small amount of glue near the base of a stamen cluster and insert the stamen into the flower from the top. Pull the stem wire down gently so that the stamen are barely visible from the outside of the flower. Apply glue to the base of a calyx and wrap it around the base of the flower. Wrap below the flower and down the stem with green floral tape. Make eight of these flowers.

To assemble the flowers, attach one flower to the tip of a 12-inch length of #18 stem wire with green floral tape. Keep adding more flowers and the four leaves as you wrap to the end of the stem wire with the tape.

CHAPTER 41

FREESIA

The freesia (of the family Iridaceae) is a South African native that originally had a pale white or cream-colored blossom. Modern hybrids, however, come in a full range of pastels. It is a long-lasting, delicate, and exquisite flower well suited to spring bouquets.

Materials

silk: white, green (optional)
cotton (optional)
starch
dyes: pink or rose, green (optional)
green cloth-covered wire: #30
cloth-covered wire to match the petals: #30
stem wire: #16, #24, #30
absorbent cotton
thin strips of tissue paper
floral tape: green
40 commercial stamen: white

Assembly

4 flowers
3 partially opened flowers
3 buds
3 leaves
10 calyxes

Following the patterns given here (figs. 41-2 through 41-7), cut twenty-four large petals, fif-

41-1. *Freesia.*

133

41-2. *Large petal.*

41-3. *Small petal.*

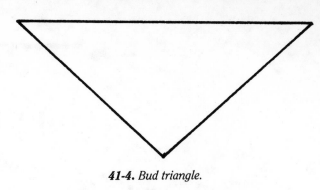

41-4. *Bud triangle.*

41-5. *Flower calyx.*

41-6. *Bud calyx.*

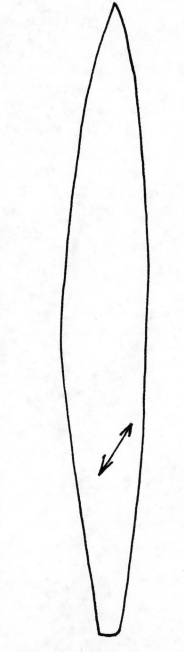

41-7. *Leaf.*

teen small petals, and three bud triangles out of starched white silk. Cut ten calyxes and three leaves out of starched white or green cotton or silk.

Dye the petals and bud triangles pink or rose. Leave the base of each petal white. Dye the leaves and calyxes green. If you wish, brush strokes of petal color onto the tips of the leaves and calyxes for accents.

Glue green cloth-covered wire along the center of each leaf, allowing 2 inches of wire to extend below the base. Glue cloth-covered wire (the same color as the petals) along the center of each large petal, allowing about 1 inch of wire to extend below the base. The small petals do not need to be wired.

Iron each leaf on the wired side with a heated knife edge, showing one long crease along the wire. Iron each large and small petal with a heated knife handle on the wired side, as shown by the *X*s in figures 41-8 and 41-9.

Make the buds first. Wrap the tip of a 2-inch length of #24 stem wire with absorbent cotton so that it looks like a cotton swab. Fold down the long edge (the base) of a bud triangle about 1 inch and slip the cotton-wrapped wire below the fold (fig. 41-10). Bring the corners of the triangle down and around and wrap them around the base of the bud. Wrap the base of the bud with #30 stem wire and twist to secure. Cut off any excess fabric below the bud to eliminate bulkiness. Wrap the base of the bud with thin strips of tissue paper and glue. Apply a small amount of glue to the base of a calyx and wrap it around the base of the bud. Wrap below the bud with narrow strips of green floral tape. (To make these narrow strips, cut the floral tape lengthwise in half. The narrow strips eliminate bulkiness in the delicate buds.) Make three of these buds.

Next make three partially opened flowers. Take a 2-inch length of #24 stem wire and wrap

41-8. *Iron each large petal at the Xs.*

about 1 inch of its tip with narrow strips of tissue paper and glue. Now apply a small amount of glue to the bases of five small petals on the ironed sides. Take three of these petals and stick them together at their bases. Attach these three petals (ironed sides inward) to the tip of the #24 stem wire (fig. 41-11). Then take two other petals, attach them together at their bases, and wrap them (ironed sides inward) around the base of the other three petals. Apply a small amount of glue to the base of a calyx and wrap it around the base of the partially opened flower (fig. 41-12). Wrap below the calyx and down the stem with narrow strips of green floral tape. Make three of these partially opened flowers.

To make a flower, you must

41-11. *Attach three petals to the tip of #24 stem wire.*

41-9. *Iron each small petal at the Xs.*

first make a stamen cluster. Take about ten white commercial stamen and cut off one of the ends. (fig. 41-13). Attach the cluster to the tip of a 2-inch length of #24 stem wire with thin strips of tissue paper and glue (fig. 41-14).

Now arrange six large petals, unwired sides inward, around the base of the stamen cluster. Wrap the base of the flower and down the stem with thin strips of tissue paper and glue. Apply a small amount of glue to the base of a calyx and wrap it around the base of the flower. Wrap below the calyx and down the stem with thin strips of green floral tape. Make four of these flowers.

To assemble everything on the main stem, start with a 20-inch length of #16 stem wire. First attach the three buds at the tip with green floral tape. Place them only about ½ inch apart and place them all on the same side of the stem wire. Next wrap on the three partially opened flowers, increasing the space

41-12. *Add two more petals and a calyx to make a partially opened flower.*

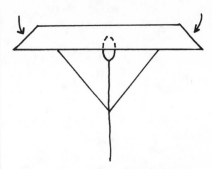

41-10. *Fold the long edge of the bud triangle over the cotton-tipped wire.*

between each one slightly after attaching them to the wire. Be sure that these flowers are placed on the same side of the stem wire as the buds. Attach the four flowers on the same side of the stem wire also. These larger flowers should be spaced about 1½ to 2 inches apart. Wrap below the flowers and down the stem with green floral tape. Add the three leaves about 3 inches below the flowers as you wrap to the end of the stem wire with the tape.

Angle all the buds and flowers out from the stem at about forty-five degrees. Then bend the main stem so that it arches gracefully, giving the impression that the stem is doing a "backbend."

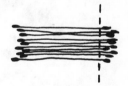

41-13. *Cut one end off of a bunch of commercial stamens.*

41-14. *Wrap each stamen cluster with tissue paper.*

CHAPTER 42

VIOLET

The violet is a member of the Violaceae family. In flower language it can have a variety of meanings—the blue violet means faithfulness or love, the sweet violet means modesty, and the purple violet means you are in my thoughts.

Materials

silk: white, green (optional), various petal colors (optional)
cotton (optional)
starch
dyes: green, various petal colors (optional)
green cloth-covered wire: #30
stem wire: #16, #24
floral tape: yellow, green
thin strips of tissue paper (optional)

Assembly

6 flowers
1 partially opened flower
7 calyxes
4 large leaves
4 small leaves

Following the patterns given here (figs. 42-2 through 42-6), cut seven *A* petals and six *B* petals out of starched silk. You can cut these petals from starched white silk and dye them purple, lav-

42-1. Violet.

42-2. *Petal A.*

42-3. *Petal B.*

42-4. *Calyx.*

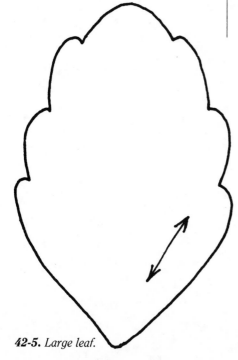

42-5. *Large leaf.*

ender, pink, or yellow, or just leave them white. If you wish to eliminate the dyeing step, you can purchase silk in the colors you need. If you choose to dye the flowers, try making the color deeper near the tip of each petal lobe, keeping the color light or white near the base. Cut four large leaves, four small leaves, and seven calyxes out of starched green silk or cotton. If green fabric is not available, you can dye these pieces.

Glue green cloth-covered wire along the center of each leaf, allowing 2 inches of wire to extend below the base. Iron each leaf with a heated knife edge on the wired side, showing a simple branching vein structure.

Iron each petal with a heated knife handle, as shown by the *X*s in figures 42-7 and 42-8.

Next make the flowers. To make the stamen, take seven 4-inch lengths of #24 stem wire and wrap their tips with a small amount of yellow floral tape to form a bulge (fig. 42-9). Below the bulge, wrap about 1 inch with thin strips of tissue paper and glue. (If your #24 wire is already cloth covered, you do not have to wrap it with tissue paper. The tissue paper is necessary with bare wire because the petals will be glued to the stem wire, and it is difficult to glue them to bare wire.) Apply a small amount of glue to the base of an *A* petal on the unironed side and attach it just below the yellow bulge, pinching its base. Now apply a small amount of glue to the base of a *B* petal on the unironed side and apply this below the yellow bulge also, pinching its base. (See fig. 42-10.) The five petals should now surround the yellow bulge. Some of the petals will overlap. Apply glue to the base of a calyx and wrap it around the stem wire below the flower (fig. 42-11). Wrap below the calyx and down the stem with green floral tape. Make six of these flowers.

Make the partially opened flower by simply applying glue to the base of an *A* petal and wrapping it tightly around a yellow stamen. Attach the calyx in the

42-7. *Iron each three-petal group at the* X*s.*

42-8. *Iron each two-petal group at the* X*s.*

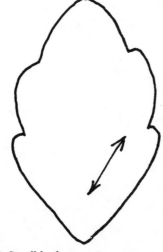

42-6. *Small leaf.*

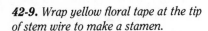

42-9. *Wrap yellow floral tape at the tip of stem wire to make a stamen.*

42-10. *Top view of petals and stamens.*

42-11. *Attach the calyx at the base of the petals.*

same way that you did with the flower and wrap the stem wire with green floral tape.

Next make a leaf spray. Take a small leaf and attach it to a 6-inch length of #24 stem wire with green floral tape. Add another small leaf, then a large

leaf, as you wrap to the end of the stem wire with the tape.

To assemble the finished flower, attach a flower to the tip of a 12-inch length of #16 stem wire with green floral tape. Add the other five flowers, the other two small leaves, and the partially opened flower as you wrap. Add

the leaf spray and the remaining three large leaves as you wrap to the end of the stem wire with green floral tape. Bend the flowers out at slight angles from the main stem.

CHAPTER 43

BLUEBELL

*T*he bluebell (of the family Liliaceae) grows from a bulb and is generally found in open grasslands, woodlands, and marshy areas. At one time bluebells were called wild hyacinths. In flower language, the bluebell can mean kindness or constancy. These flowers brighten up many spring bouquets and also make fine wedding flowers.

Materials
silk: white
cotton (optional)
starch
dyes: green, blue
green cloth-covered wire: #30
thread: blue
stem wire: #18, #24
18 commercial stamen: white
floral tape: green

Assembly
6 flowers
3 leaves

Following the patterns given here (figs 43-2 and 43-3), cut six petal sets out of starched white silk. Cut three leaves out of starched silk or cotton.
Dye the petal sets blue. Deepen the color at the base of the flower. Dye the leaves green.

43-1. Bluebell.

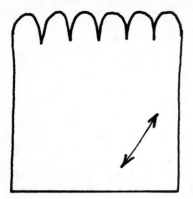

43-2. *Petal set.*

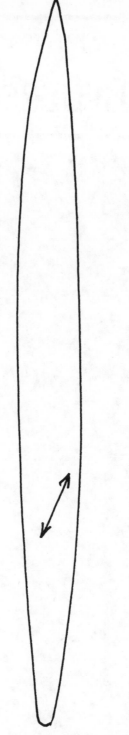

43-3. *Leaf.*

43-4. *Iron each petal set at the Xs.*

43-5. *Gather the base of each petal set around the stamen cluster.*

Glue green cloth-covered wire along the center of each leaf, allowing about 2 inches of wire to extend below the base.

Iron each leaf with a heated knife edge, showing one lengthwise crease along the wire on the wired side. Iron the tips of each petal set with a heated knife handle, as shown by the *X*s in figure 43-4.

Sew wide running stitches very close to the base of each petal set. Later you will pull this thread to gather the base of the flower around the stamen.

Make six stamen clusters. Make the first one at the tip of an 18-inch length of #18 stem wire. Cut the ends off of three white commercial stamen and attach them to the tip of the wire with green floral tape. Make the other five stamen clusters at the tips of five 4-inch lengths of #24 stem wire.

Form each petal set into a cylinder by gluing the sides together. Make sure the flower tips radiate outward. Apply a small amount of glue to the base of the flower on the inside of the cylinder and insert a stamen cluster. Pull the thread at the base of the flower to gather the flower around the stamen (fig. 43-5). Wrap the base of the flower and down the stem with green floral tape. Make six of these flowers.

To arrange the flowers on the main stem, start with the flower at the tip of the #18 stem wire and continue wrapping with green floral tape. Attach all the other flowers, seam sides down, at 2-inch intervals. The last two flowers should have slightly longer stems than the other four. All of the flowers should appear to be on the same plane. Continue wrapping below all the flowers with green floral tape and add the three leaves at various places along the stem. Wrap to the end of the wire with the tape. Bend all the flower stems so the flowers droop slightly.

CHAPTER 44

CHRYSANTHEMUM

*T*he chrysanthemum (of the family Compositae) can be either perennial or annual. In flower language, a yellow chrysanthemum means slighted love, white means truth, and red means I love you.

Materials
silk: white, green (optional)
cotton (optional)
starch
dyes: yellowish green, various
    petal colors, green (optional)
green cloth-covered wire: #30
stem wire: #16
floral tape: yellow, green

Assembly
1 flower
3 leaves
2 calyxes

Following the patterns given here (figs. 44-2 through 44-4), cut four petal circles out of starched white silk. Cut three leaves and two calyxes out of starched white or green silk or cotton.

Dye the center of each petal yellowish green. Dye the circumference of each petal yellow, pink, orange, or red, or leave it white. If you are using white fabric, dye the leaves and calyxes green.

44-1. Chrysanthemum.

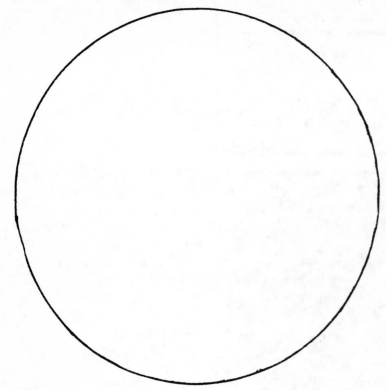

44-2. *Petal circle.*

44-3. *Calyx.*

Glue green cloth-covered wire along the center of each leaf and each leaf lobe, allowing 2 inches of wire to extend below the base. (see fig. 44-5.)

Fold a petal circle in half to form a semicircle. With small, sharp scissors, cut around the semicircle to form long petal lobes (fig. 44-6). Unfold the petal circle. Cut the remaining petal circles in this manner.

44-4. *Leaf.*

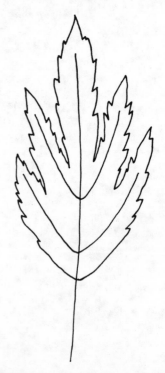

44-5. *Add two extra wires to each leaf for support.*

44-6. *Cut petals from a semicircle.*

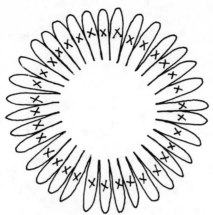

44-7. *Iron each petal circle at the Xs.*

44-8. *Iron each calyx at the Xs.*

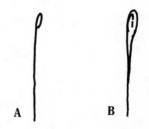

44-9. (A) *Bend a piece of #16 stem wire into a loop.* (B) *Wrap the loop with yellow floral tape.*

Iron the petals and calyxes with a heated knife handle, as shown by the *X*s in figures 44-7 and 44-8. Iron each leaf on the wired side with a heated knife edge, showing a simple branching vein structure on each lobe of the leaf.

Next make the flower. Take a 12-inch length of #16 stem wire and bend the tip to form a small hook (fig. 44-9A). Wrap the hook with yellow floral tape (fig. 44-9B). Now pierce the center of each petal circle with an awl on the ironed side. Apply a small amount of glue around the hole on the ironed side. Insert the stem wire through the hole on the ironed side. Slide the petal circle up and pinch its base below

the yellow floral tape. Do the same with the remaining three petal circles, applying glue and sliding them up and pinching their bases below the tip of the stem wire.

Now pierce the ironed side of the calyx in the center with an awl, apply glue near the hole on the ironed side, and slide the calyx up and pinch it below the flower. Attach the other calyx right below the first one so that their sepals are alternate. Wrap

below the flower and down the stem with green floral tape. Add the three leaves as you wrap to the end of the stem wire with the tape.

CHAPTER 45

IVY LEAVES

*I*vy leaves provide bulk and contrast to floral bouquets. They work well in wedding bouquets and table centerpieces.

Materials
silk: green
starch
green cloth-covered wire: #30
stem wire: #20
floral tape: green

Assembly
5 small leaves
4 medium-small leaves
3 medium leaves
3 large leaves

Following the patterns given here (figs. 45-2 through 45-5), cut the leaves out of starched green silk. Cut out five small leaves, four medium-small leaves, three medium leaves, and three large leaves.

On the large leaves, glue green cloth-covered wire along the center and add two extra wires for support (fig. 45-6). The medium and small leaves are easier to wire. Just glue the green cloth-covered wire along their centers. Be sure to allow about 3 inches of wire to extend below the base of each leaf.

45-1. *Ivy leaves.*

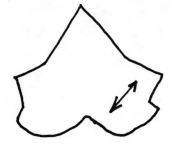

45-2. *Small leaf.*

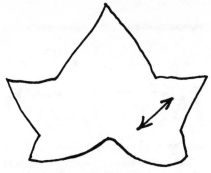

45-3. *Medium-small leaf.*

45-4. *Medium leaf.*

45-5. *Large leaf.*

45-6. *Add two extra wires to support each large leaf.*

Iron each leaf on the wired side with a heated knife edge, showing a compound branching vein structure.

Arrange the leaves on the #20 stem wire. Start with the small leaves. Attach them to the tip of the stem wire with green floral tape and space them about ½ inch apart. Then add the medium-small leaves, increasing the space between them slightly. Add the medium leaves next, then the large leaves, increasing the space between sizes of leaves as you continue to wrap with green floral tape. Wrap to the end of the stem wire with the tape.

CHAPTER 46

MAPLE LEAVES

Autumn maple leaves are often used in fall bouquets and table centerpieces. They provide a neutral background to an arrangement, providing contrast to bright flowers.

Materials
silk: white
starch
dyes: orange or yellow, brown
brown cloth-covered wire: #30
floral tape: brown
stem wire: #18

Assembly
4 large leaves
5 small leaves

Following the patterns given here (figs 46-2 and 46-3), cut four large leaves and five small ones out of starched white silk. Dye them brown, then accent the edges on one side with orange or yellow dye.

Glue three pieces of brown cloth-covered wire along each large leaf, as shown in figure 46-4. Glue brown cloth-covered wire along the center of each small leaf. Be sure to allow about 3 inches of wire to extend below the base of each leaf. Now wrap all the leaf stems with brown floral tape.

46-1. *Maple leaves.*

146

Iron each leaf on the wired side, showing a compound branching vein structure.

To assemble the leaves, start with a small one. Attach it to the tip of an 18-inch length of #18 stem wire. Keep wrapping with brown floral tape, using all the small leaves first. Leave about 1½ inches between leaves, allowing some of the wrapped leaf-stem wire to show. After the small leaves are attached to the main stem, add the large leaves. Continue wrapping to the end of the stem wire with brown floral tape.

46-2. Large leaf.

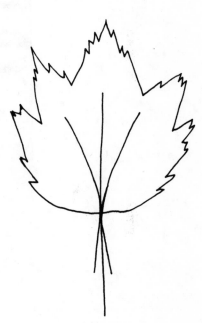

46-4. Add two extra wires to support each large leaf.

46-3. Small leaf.

· PART III ·
WEDDING FLOWERS

CHAPTER 47

BOUQUETS

*T*he flowers carried by the bride and bridesmaids require the most attention, time, and effort, so be particularly careful to select colors and sizes of flowers that coordinate with your design and color scheme.

Start with a color wheel, which provides a guide to the range of color choices available. Find your wedding-dress color on the wheel. The colors on each side of your dress color are suitable. So are complementary colors, which appear exactly opposite your wedding-dress color on the wheel. Decide whether to use matching colors, blending colors, contrasting colors, or a combination of these in your arrangements. Be sure to choose two or three different colors to avoid monotony.

First select two or three types of main flowers. These should be flowers of medium size but of different shapes—such as the rose, the carnation, the lily, and the orchid. Next choose two or three types of smaller filler flowers, such as miniature orchids, rosebuds, buttercups, or stephanotis.

Assemble the main flowers first, then add the fillers. The stems should all appear to originate from the same point. A secondary color near the center of the bouquet helps provide a focal point that is appealing. To bring out the beauty of your arrangement, green foliage is a must. While assembling, remember not to crowd and overwork the flowers—a delicate, airy look often works best and will enhance the beauty of the individual flowers.

Nosegays

The nosegay is a hand-held bouquet that is merely a round arrangement of flowers without extra sprays (fig. 47-1). If you wish, you can support the nosegay with a circlet of lace (available at craft and card shops). Ribbon bows and streamers attached to the base of the bouquet with thin wire add an attractive touch.

Cascades

The cascade is simply a nosegay with a spray that trails below the center of the bouquet (fig. 47-2). Plan the size of a cascade carefully, because it can be overwhelming if it is too exten-sive. The distance from the center of the bouquet to its bottom tip should measure no more than half the bouquet's width.

47-1. Nosegay.

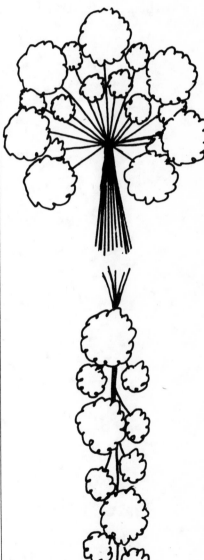

47-2. Cascade.

Arm Arrangements

Designed to rest along the length of the forearm, an arm arrangement is easy to create. It is usually linear in shape, with considerable tall, flat foliage, such as sword fern. Ribbon and streamers add special elegance (fig. 47-3).

Duplicate Bouquet

After putting so much care and effort into the bridal bouquet, it is sad to think it will be thrown to the crowd during the wedding celebration. Silk flowers allow an

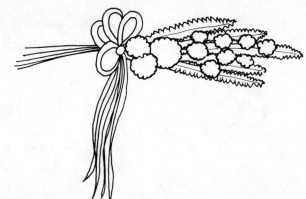

47-3. Arm arrangement.

easy solution. Make an additional bridal bouquet—a smaller, simpler version of the arrangement

—so the bride can enjoy her special silk wedding bouquet for years to come.

CHAPTER 48

CORSAGES, BOUTONNIERES, AND COMBS

*O*ther important members of the wedding party need flowers to designate their roles in the ceremony. These body flowers —corsages, boutonnieres, and sometimes combs—are easy and fun to make. The most important rule to remember is to keep them simple. Often just a single flower with foliage backing is the most appealing solution.

Boutonnieres

The groom often wears a boutonniere that echoes the bride's floral arrangement. Groomsmen often wear boutonnieres that match the bouquets carried by the bride's attendants.

Start with foliage backing, which you must remember to keep flat. You might want to purchase a sprig of ready-made silk fern—or you can make your own foliage. Add a single small flower, such as a rosebud, stephanotis, or carnation. If you wish, add a bit of dried baby's breath for accent, but no ribbons or bows. Secure the boutonniere to the lapel with an ordinary straight pin.

Corsages

It is also important to keep a corsage simple, although more than one type of flower may be used for a corsage.

Start again with foliage backing, which you must keep flat. Silk fern or rose leaves provide good foliage backing. If you wish, add a bit of dried baby's breath. Then wrap on an odd number of flowers, using floral tape that matches the flower colors. Wrap on no more than five flowers. You might use rosebuds, stephanotis, miniature orchids, or cherry blossoms. An especially beautiful and simple corsage is made from a single phalaenopsis orchid with a bit of dried baby's breath. Add a bow near the base of the corsage, but do not use ribbon streamers.

Combs

A floral comb is an easy wedding arrangement to make—and it can be used again for other special occasions.

Start with a plastic comb and attach foliage backing directly to it with clear glue. Keep the foliage flat and wrap on a few small flowers with floral tape that matches the flower colors.

CHAPTER 49

LONG-STEMMED ROSE

*T*he bride or other members of the wedding party may wish to carry a single long-stemmed rose. Though simple, it looks very elegant and is especially easy to make if you have practiced making silk roses (Chapter 7). You can provide a personal hand-made look if you roll the edges of the rose petals. (See "Rolled-Edge Flowers" in Chapter 2.)

Follow the patterns and instructions in Chapter 7, but cut the calyx and leaves from starched lace (white for the calyx and green for the leaves). Wrap the leaf stems with satin ribbon and glue and wrap below the calyx and down the main stem with satin ribbon and glue. Attach the leaves and a few ribbon streamers as you wrap to the end of the main stem wire with the ribbon. To make the rose even more realistic, add a scent to it. (See "The Reality Factor" in Chapter 2.)

CHAPTER 50

COLOR GUIDE TO WEDDING FLOWERS

*T*he following list is designed to help you select wedding flowers to match your color scheme. The list includes both main flowers and smaller filler flowers. Keep in mind that the list is not exhaustive—and you can even change the colors of flowers to unconventional shades. For example, consider a blue buttercup or yellow stephanotis if these flowers happen to be just the right shape or size for your arrangement. That's the beauty of making your own silk flowers— the possibilities are exciting and limitless.

Color	Main Flowers	Filler Flowers
yellow	rose, carnation, chrysanthemum, daffodil, sweet pea, tiger lily	rose buds, buttercups, stephanotis, carnation buds
orange	poppy, rose, tiger lily, sweet pea, rhododendron, azalea, nasturtium	rose buds, sweet pea buds, carnation buds
dusty pink	rose, carnation, lily, phalaenopsis orchid, camellia, rhododendron	mini-orchid, partially opened cherry blossoms, lilac, rose buds, carnation buds
blue	pansy, sweet pea, iris, morning glory	cornflower, forget-me-not, lilac, blue bells
red	poinsettia, hibiscus, geranium, camellia, rose, carnation	rose buds, carnation buds, individual geranium florets

Color	Main Flowers	Filler Flowers
lavender	iris, morning glory, sweet pea, azalea	bluebells, forget-me-not, lilac, fuchsia, violets
burgundy	pansy, rose, carnation, camellia, cattleya, phalaenopsis orchid	rose buds, carnation buds, lilac, stephanotis, cherry blossoms, violets

METRIC CONVERSION CHART

Metric Conversion Chart

⅛ inch = 0.32 cm
¼ inch = 0.64 cm
½ inch = 1.27 cm
¾ inch = 1.91 cm
1 inch   = 2.54 cm
1 foot   = 30.48 cm
1 square foot = 0.09 square m
1 square yard = 0.84 square m

BIBLIOGRAPHY

Books

Ash, Beryl, and Anthony Dyson. *Introducing Dyeing and Printing.* New York: Watson-Guptill Publications, 1970.

Cocker, Henry, and Ippolito Pizzetti. *Flowers: A Guide to Your Garden.* New York: Harry N. Abrams, Inc., 1968.

Gorer, Richard. *The Development of Garden Flowers.* Gateshead, Great Britain: Eyre and Spottiswoode Ltd., 1970.

Hamazaki, Yasuko. *Lovely Paper Flowers.* Tokyo: Ondozisha Publishers, 1977.

Iida, Miyuki and Tomoko. *The Art of Handmade Flowers.* Tokyo, New York, San Francisco: Kodansha International Ltd., 1971.

Jeffery, Vera, and Malcolm Lewis. *The Flower Workshop.* New York: Hearst, 1980.

Kramer, Jack. *Natural Dyes, Plants and Processes.* New York: Charles Scribner's Sons, 1972.

Powell, Claire. *The Meaning of Flowers—A Garland of Plant Lore and Symbolism from Popular Custom and Literature.* London: Jupiter Books, Ltd., 1977.

Shuttleworth, Floyd, Herbert Zim, and Gordon Dillon. *Orchids.* New York: Golden Press, 1970.

Uchiyama, Yuri. *Ribbon Flowers, Paper Flowers.* Tokyo: Kodansha International Ltd., 1974.

Pamphlets

Eidick, Mary. *Lovely Silk Flowers.* Rosemead, California: Craft Course Publishers, 1976.

Gilbert, Glenn. *Soft and Silky: Home Decor with Pretty Petals.* New York: SEI Craft Publications, 1978.

Hammond, Andrew. *Beginner's Guide for Wedding Florals.* Little Rock, Arkansas: Leisure Art, Inc., 1983.

How to Make Your Own Wedding Flowers. Omaha, Nebraska: Harold Mangelsen and Sons, Inc., 1982.

Rutecki, Dottie. *From Silk to Flowers*. Danville, Illinois: Pat Depke, Inc., 1977.

Suszczynski, Marjorie. *Flowering Silk—The Easy Way to Make Silk Flowers*. Norcross, Georgia: Designers Artistic Crafts, Inc., 1978.

Trick, Burt and Patty. *Tricks of Arranging Silks . . . for Weddings*. Santa Maria, California: Trick, Inc., 1982.

Valle, Betty. *Sweet and Simple Silk Weddings*. Norcross, Georgia: Plaid Enterprises, Inc., 1979.

INDEX

A

Anemone, 13, 97–99
Arm arrangements, 152
Assembly of flowers, 11–12
Azalea, 66–68

B

Bindweed, *see* Oriental morning
    glory
Black-eyed Susan, 118–21
Bluebell, 139–40
Bougainvillea, 85–86
Bouquets, 151–52
Boutonnieres, 153
Buds, how to make, 11
Buttercup, 112–14, 151

C

Camellia, 57–59
Carnation, 17–19, 151
Cascades, 151
Cattleya, 44–47
Cherry blossom, 82–84
Chrysanthemum, 141–43
    See also Marguerite
Colors, choosing, 8, 151
Combs, 153
Coneflowers, *see* Black-eyed
    Susan
Cornflower, 110–11
Corsages, 153
Cymbidium orchid, 51–53

D

Daffodil, 35–37
Day lily, 115–17
Digitalis, 87–93
Dogwood, 103–104
Dyes, and dyeing, 5, 7–8, 13

F

Fabrics, appropriate types, 4, 12
Flower centers, 3–4
Forget-me-not, 105–106
Foxglove, *see* Digitalis
Freesia, 133–35
Fuchsia, 100–102

G

Gardenia, 41–43
Geraniums, 12, 75–77
Gillyflower, *see* Carnation
Gladiolus, 8, 78–81
Glue, and gluing, 8–9

H

Heating tools, 9
Hibiscus, 13, 26–28

I

Iris, 13, 38–40
Ironing silk flowers, tools for, 3
Ivy leaves, 144–45

L

Lilacs, 12, 107–109
Lilies, *see* Day lily; Tiger lily

M

Madagascar jasmine, *see* Stephan-
    otis
Mallow, *see* Hibiscus
Maple leaves, 146–47
Marguerite, 72–74
Mass production, 6
Morning glory, 8
    See also Oriental morning
    glory; Wild morning glory

Moth orchid, *see* Phalaenopsis
    orchid

N

Narcissus, 35, 37
Nasturtium, 20–22
Nosegays, 151

O

Orchids, 151
    cattleya, 44–47
    cymbidium, 51–53
    miniature, 54–56, 151
    phalaenopsis, 48–50
Oriental morning glory, 122–26
Oriental poppy, 13, 94–96

P

Pansy, 23–25
Patterns, cutting, 6–7
Pistil, how to make, 3
Poinsettia, 60–62

R

Rhododendron, 63–65
Rolled-edges, how to make, 13–
    14
Rose, 29–31, 151
    long-stemmed, 154
    small climbing, 32–34
Rose mallow, *see* Hibiscus

S

Scenting flowers, 14
Shaping flower parts, 9–10
Silk, natural production of, 1
Spotting leaves and petals, 13
Stamens, how to make, 3, 10–11

Starch or sizing, 5, 7
Stephanotis, 131–35, 151
Supplies, source, 3
Sweet pea, 8, 11, 69–71

T
Tendrils, how to make, 11
Tiger lily, 115–17

Tools and materials, 3–5
Tulips, 5

V
Veins, ironing onto leaves, 9, 10
Violet, 136–38

W
Waved edges, how to make, 13
Wedding flowers, 149–56
Wild hyacinths, *see* Bluebell
Wild morning glory, 127–30
Wire, 7
Wrinkled petals, how to make, 13